CE

Pakistan's Trade with Eastern Bloc Countries

Michael Kidron

The Praeger Special Studies program—
utilizing the most modern and efficient book
production techniques and a selective
worldwide distribution network—makes
available to the academic, government, and
business communities significant, timely
research in U.S. and international economic, social, and political development.

Pakistan's Trade with Eastern Bloc Countries

PRAEGER SPECIAL STUDIES IN INTERNATIONAL ECONOMICS AND DEVELOPMENT

Praeger Publishers   New York   Washington   London

PRAEGER PUBLISHERS
111 Fourth Avenue, New York, N.Y. 10003, U.S.A.
5, Cromwell Place, London S.W.7, England

Published in the United States of America in 1972
by Praeger Publishers, Inc.

Library of Congress Catalog Card Number: 77-176397

Printed in the United States of America

To the memory of
The Pakistan Institute of Development Economics
Karachi, 1957-Dacca, March 25, 1971

This study started as an offshoot of a larger work on Russian aid and trade in South Asia, financed by the (British) Social Science Research Council. It has been made possible as a separate study by the generosity of the Ford Foundation, which sustained me in Pakistan and at the Pakistan Institute of Development Economics.

The East of the Introduction is a looser concept than the Eastern Bloc Countries (or EBC's, of the main text) that comprises China, Russia, and East Europe (Albania, Bulgaria, Czechoslovakia, East Germany, Hungary, Romania, Poland, and Yugoslavia). The definition is slightly arbitrary in including Yugoslavia, an important trading partner, but not Cuba, Mongolia, North Korea, or North Vietnam, whose presence would have made little difference to the results while adding substantially to the work. Unless explicitly stated East Europe does not include Russia. The South of the Introduction stands for what one variously called the "underdeveloped," "less developed," "developing," or "backward" countries in Asia, Africa, and Latin America.

Except for matters of detail, the main text was completed in mid-March 1971, before Pakistan took its new and fateful course. It was finally finished in May. The Introduction followed later, in early September, at the Publisher's behest.

ACKNOWLEDGMENTS

The core of this study has been exceptionally labor-intensive and has taxed the time and patience of many people in Pakistan and Oxford. A number of research assistants at the now-defunct Pakistan Institute of Development Economics (PIDE) put a great deal of effort into compiling and processing the raw data on which it is based. These were Mohammed Aslam and Pervez Aslam Shami, and, briefly, Maudood Mirza. Others, specially recruited for the work were Ali Ahmad, Hazoor Ahmad, Syed Zahur, Hasan Rizvi, and Azhar Javed. Ali Ahmad acted as informal convenor for the entire team over a number of months and subsequently gathered up many loose threads on his own.

PIDE staff economists Abdur Razak Kemal and Mohammed Faiz were also involved, the former acting as convenor in the initial stages; and Rhoda Sanjana, secretary to the Yale-Pakistan Project at PIDE, and Shabih Haidar, personal assistant to the director, were essential links with the world at large.

In Oxford, at the Institute of Commonwealth Studies, Akbar and Barbro Noman, my and his research assistant respectively, sustained the laborious task of giving final shape to the larger tables. Paul Gerhardt collected material for the Introduction and Peter Balacs helped in passing. Frances Stewart cut through many of the knots in an early draft and materially improved the presentation.

That is as to labor. The land was opened up by a concourse of people whose extent is as embarrassing to me as individual mention might be to them. Officials at the Planning Commission and the Provincial Planning Divisions, the Central Statistical Office, the State Bank of Pakistan, the Ministries of Commerce, of Finance, and of Industries, the Economic Affairs Division, as well as in autonomous government corporations and agencies too numerous to mention bore a heavy load of questioning and cross-questioning with patience and frankness. Only at the Ministry of Commerce, and only after a first draft had been read, was there any attempt to erase a memory or a phrase, particularly those relating to named countries and, among these, to China above all.

Eastern trade officials were also generous with their time and interest in most cases, although, it ought to be said, the Chinese were unapproachable and the Russians more generous with my time than their interest, asking me to take my questions to Islamabad when in Karachi, to Moscow when in Islamabad, and to Geneva when in Moscow.

Businessmen and their organizations were unfailingly courteous and forthcoming. And my colleagues at PIDE acted as the best of colleagues do—ever helpful, ever patient.

CONTENTS

PART II

APPENDIXES

Pakistan's Trade with Eastern Bloc Countries

East-South trade grew rapidly between the mid-1950's and the mid-1960's; faltered for a couple of years, during 1967 and 1968; and then resumed its upward course. In the 1960's it remained the fastest-growing component of world trade: twice as fast as West-South trade; twice as fast as the East's or South's intratrades; and faster, though only marginally so, than the two other rapidly rising flows— East-West trade and the intratrade of the industrial West.

During that decade the South absorbed more than 25 percent of the growth in the East's exports; and though the East was hardly so important a market for the South, it did take slightly more than 6 percent of the latter's growth in exports (10 percent if mineral fuels are excluded). By 1969 the share of East-South trade as a proportion of world trade had more than doubled, rising from 1.1 to 2.3 percent. Of the increase, 40 percent came through the expansion of trade between the handful of major trading partners of the late 1950's—India, Egypt, and Hong Kong on the one hand, and Russia and China on the other; some of it came from an extension of trade to a large number of new ones. In both cases it was linked to the use of special trade-promoting instruments.

The most distinctive of these is the long-term bilateral trading agreement, or barter agreement, that now covers 50-60 percent of East Europe's—and 90 percent of Russia's—trade with the South. Normally it sets quantitative targets for the major traded commodities, as 80 percent of Russia's bilateral agreements do; it stipulates that trade should balance more or less each year and that settlement should be in the currency of the Southern partner. In this way the key agreements tend to create fixed, identifiable markets for certain goods while insulating them from world trade.

Not all of the agreements do this. Some set out only the most general conditions of trade, or list goods without setting targets of any kind; and some specify payment in convertible currencies. But these have proved to be fairly weak instruments that do little more than establish the partners as potential "vents" for each other without safeguarding them from imbalance in trade and payments.[1] Nor are all targets sacrosanct. Many are never achieved and most are insured against nonfulfilment—all EBC's and many of their Southern trading partners take great pains to keep open more than one line of supply for themselves and to shut off competing lines to their own.

3

It has sometimes been difficult to conclude bilateral trading agreements. In many Southern countries the private sector has been suspicious from the start, less of the proposed Eastern trading partners than of the additional leverage the agreements give to their own government officials; while for their part, the officials have often found their Western-oriented exporters or importers reluctant to break new ground or to give up the advantages unofficially associated with having access to convertible currencies.

Under the circumstances and despite their real need not to stray far from world prices however defined, the EBC's have had to pay to enter the market. There is no saying how heavily. Neither set of partners is interested in publishing the fact of deviation from such prices, let alone the degree of deviation; and bilateralism itself tends to obscure the real level of the prices paid in any one direction. But on the partial evidence adduced in Chapter 4, corroborated elsewhere,[2] on the evidence too of the constant run of complaints from Eastern trading organizations about price discrimination,[3] the entry fee has been high, the more so as the EBC's compete fiercely against each other.

It has also not always been easy to maintain bilateral trading once achieved. Most of the partners are economically small. All are unstable, prone to fluctuations in the price and production parameters on which the trade targets rest. They are tempted to, and often do, set unrealistic goals for exports (or imports) in order to sustain the flow of needed imports (or exports). In many cases unwanted goods are either absorbed unwillingly and at the cost of recriminatory negotiations in the next round, or switch-traded in contravention of the terms of most agreements (as is shown at some length in Chapter 1) with similar consequences. Quality undertakings have not been honored, and so on. Bilateralism itself, through its insistence on maintaining an equality between annual exports and imports for each pair of partners has tended to restrict the growth of trade beyond narrow limits.

The partners have tended to meet these difficulties in one or both of two ways: by vesting the bilateral arrangements with some flexibility or by building, particularly in the South, a set of institutional buttresses.

The first—flexibility—has been attempted through the use of swing credits; extending the period of settlement; buying in bulk at the right seasons rather than at times of maximum bureaucratic convenience, including unscheduled items and changing quotas during

the currency of an agreement; shifting from quantitative to global
value targets; and even modifying the traditional (Eastern) concept of
a foreign trade plan as being a predetermined volume of trade. There
have been experiments in triangular clearing (Russia-Indonesia-India
for example, or Egypt-Hungary-Bulgaria) and some progress toward
an East-South multilateralism based on a transferable ruble. There
has even been serious talk, in some of the smaller East European
countries, of free trade based on existing convertible currencies.

However, since real flexibility is difficult to attain for poor
countries plagued by reserve and balance-of-payments difficulties,
particularly when they do not share common prices or a common
pricing system, the prime response has been in laying down a
supportive institutional matrix. In the South the agreements have
been accompanied by the establishment of state trading organizations.
In the East, where state trading has existed from the start, there has
been a rush of new design and consultancy organizations that tend to
specialize in exporting know-how to the South; special, mainly techno-
logical, teaching institutions to cater to students from the South; and
so on. In both, joint marketing organizations have been set up to
operate in third countries. There are joint shipping lines, joint
production arrangements, product-sharing agreements, and mixed
companies.

More far-reaching in principle, although not very effective in
practice, are the mixed economic commissions at the ministerial
level that are intended to supervise the trade and other agreements,
to encourage the development of export industries geared to each
other's needs, to exercise joint production planning, and generally to
orchestrate the full range of economic contact between the partners.
This might amount to partial coordination of national plans as in the
case of Russia and Romania and Iran, or Czechoslovakia and India,
or in that of a number of East European and Middle Eastern countries.
Together with a strong lacing of credit the mixed economic commissions might even encourage national planning as such, as in some
African countries. Logically, and assuming no countervailing influences, they should lead to full coordination, but there is little evidence
to date of that having happened—trade agreements have not generally
coincided with the preparation of long- or medium-term plans on
either side.

Barter agreements and the new institutions associated with
them have done a great deal to locate existing surpluses and direct
them toward mutual trade. They cannot by themselves generate a
substantial increase in their volume. For that, and indeed in order

to sustain some of the new institutions themselves, new resources are required, which is where the second major trade promotion instrument comes in—the credit or "economic and technical cooperation" agreement.

Since the mid-1950's, sixty countries have concluded such agreements with East Europe, of which forty have been with Russia, the major source by far; and some $14.5 billion of credit has been advanced to them (1955-67), $5.5 billion on military account, almost entirely from Russia.[4] Some of these agreements have followed on ordinary commercial agreements, some have accompanied them, and some—the 1955 Egyptian arms credit, for example—have been a precondition for them. All have resulted in a substantial increase in the volume of trade.

They are ideally suited to doing so. All credits are tied to source and most nonmilitary credits to individual projects or project-oriented national plans. Most of the latter—67 percent in the case of Russia, 75 percent in that of Czechoslovakia—finances the import of plant and machinery, and a large proportion of this—67 percent in the case of Russia—is in the form of complete plants. Since the over-whelming part of Eastern arms supplies are "major weapons" of some complexity (ships, aircraft, armored fighting vehicles, and missiles), and since project credits are also normally for large, fairly complex "core" plants in the state sector, they tend to induce a secondary demand for educational, technical, and managerial services during installation, and a continuing demand for replacements, parts, and other inputs (including ammunition) thereafter. Finally, since all but a minute fraction of such credits are serviced and repaid in goods, their direct effect on trade can be, and has been, considerable.

There is no secret made about these effects. In Poland extend-ing credit has been pronounced to be the "only correct method of expanding our foreign trade with the underdeveloped countries."[5] In Russia, economists have used a form of credit-ruble trade multi-plier to estimate the number of "rubles of trade per ruble of credit extended"[6] and attribute the fast growth of Russian trade with the South compared with that of East-Europe to its overwhelming predom-inance as a creditor, for "credits, especially long-term ones . . . lead to increased import demands (correspondingly, they give rise to an increase in the exports of socialist countries)."[7]

Credits are not granted exclusively to increase trade nor in many cases primarily to do so. Even when they are they quickly get lost in an interlocking network of other purposes—compared and adjusted for size, "softness," flexibility, and so on with their Western (or Chinese) competitors; annexed as weapons by the realpolitik-als and as "aid" by the propagandists; exploited by the bureaucrats to extend their institutional territory and interests. In short, they gain a significance that stretches well beyond the mundanities of commerce. Yet their primary links are to trade creation and expansion, and the judgement as to whether they are high political instruments or not must rest on a larger view of East-South trade and economic relations.

In a technical sense these relations are always political since they flow from decisions taken by governments and are justified in political terms. They are often clearly political in a larger sense too, for many of the commodities bought by the East are marginal to its needs, and there is not much strictly economic rationale for heavy arms buying by the South or for the feverish competition between Russia and China to establish links with places as far apart as the Sudan or the Philippines, or as unlikely as Thailand.

However, often what seems to be purely political is so only in the short term and ultimately becomes economic;[8] and even where time does not perform that particular alchemy, both sides would find it punitively expensive to sustain a political association that remained for long at variance with their economic interests. By the early 1960's Russia and the East-European countries were clearly beginning to count, and reject, the cost of purely political trade.[9]

Assuming then that the directly political component of trade is marginal both to its current volume and to the direction it is likely to take over the long term, the prospect for East-South trade must be assessed on economic grounds.

The East's foreign trade is almost certain to continue its rapid recent growth. The EBC's are still among the fastest-growing economies in the world, expanding as a group some 25 percent as fast again as the West during the 1960's. They also include some of the developed world's most unbalanced economies whose continued expansion depends increasingly on gaining access to outside technology and materials. Since this need is coinciding with the dismantling of many of the West's restrictions on Eastern trade; since the many institutional and doctrinal adjustments to such trade that have been made—including economic reform and the recognition of comparative advantage as a valid principle—are exerting an effect of their own; and since the external and internal pressures for high growth rates show no signs of abating, the outlook is for a substantial increase in foreign trade in general, notwithstanding the strong drag exercised by bureaucratic planning, the monopoly of foreign trade, Russia's renewed attempt to act as the intermediary between East-Europe and the West, and a host of other factors.

Some of the growth in trade is bound to find its way directly to the South. Certainly it is meant to. At the end of the 1960's Eastern economists were projecting a two-way trade between the CMEA (Council for Mutual Economic Assistance) countries (excluding inter alia China and Yugoslavia) and the South (including Yugoslavia but not China) of $16 billion by 1980, nearly three times the 1967 total and representing a compound growth rate of 8.6 percent per year.[10] By then 25 percent or more of Russia's foreign trade is expected to be with the South, compared with a little over 17 percent in 1968 (and 3.3 percent in 1960). A large, although unstated, proportion of the East's imports is expected to be of manufactures compared with the 15 percent of 1968, and naturally the expansion of trade is expected to proceed smoothly.

In terms of what was actually achieved in the 1960's, these are unambitious targets: East-South trade grew at 13 percent per year in the middle years and by slightly more than 7 percent per year overall; the South's sales of manufactures and semimanufactures to the East more than trebled in the first half of the decade and then doubled again in the second half, to form 13 percent or so of the total at the end.

But the 1960's were exceptional in many ways. The Sino-Soviet break diverted a significant proportion of intra-East trade southward—as much as 20 percent of foreign trade in China's case. The last major bloc of European colonies—in Africa—assumed national status, which added to the number of trading partners and hastened the process already underway, of substituting direct dealing for trading through international commodity markets via Western intermediaries. The 1960's also saw the first significant, although largely abortive, attempts at economic reform in the East, which led to increased international trade both directly, (as was intended) and indirectly via the attempts by some of the East European countries to ride trade toward greater independence of Russia. It was a decade in which embargoes on East-West trade eroded rapidly. Finally, the 1960's started with so low a level of trade between the two sets of partners that the most modest absolute increases were bound to look impressive in terms of relative growth. At the end of the decade, East-South trade was still only 9 percent of West-South trade despite its having grown more than twice as fast in the period; and exports of manufactures from the South to the East, which had grown a third as fast again as such exports to the West, were less than 7 percent of their value.

There is little point in discussing whether or not the increase in trade was adequate to the South's needs. EBC economists themselves claim no more than that it cushioned the relative decline in the South's traditional outlets,[11] a claim borne out by the dullness of the South's terms of trade throughout the decade.[12] Two points, however, should be made: It was larger than anything envisaged for the future, and it failed to achieve its targets.

On a sober assessment of prospects, overall volume fell short of the forecasts current in the early 1960's by 20 percent. On a more euphoric view the shortfall was as much as 50 percent.[13] The commodity composition of trade changed, but remained firmly within an "imperialist" mold: Crude materials, food, and beverages still accounted for 85 percent of the South's exports to the East at the end of the decade, twice their weight in exports to the West. Exports of manufactures were encouraged and in fact grew twice as fast as all exports to the East, so that the 7:1 ratio of primary goods to manufactures at the end of the decade was more or less the same for exports to both wings of the developed world. But they were markedly more raw-materials-based in the case of exports to the East—traditional textile products like jute bags, linens, ribbons, carpets, fishnets, etc., made up 50 percent of manufactured exports to the EBC's compared with just over 20 percent to the West. Russia and East Europe's exports to the South were in the same mold. They were more concentrated on manufactures than were the West's; and within manufactures, four times more biased toward armaments, today's nonproductive equivalent of nineteenth century Lancashire's cotton shrouds.[14]

Similarly with the geographical dispersal of trade. Despite the fillip provided by the emergence of new trading partners, East-South trade showed little sign of breaking beyond the narrow confines with which it entered the decade: The five major Southern partners (India, Egypt, Hong Kong, Pakistan, and Turkey) which accounted for 71 percent of the total in 1960, provided 75 percent in 1969.[15] And so too with stability. East-South trade proved as erratic in practice as the South's traditionally unstable trade with the West.[16]

Some of these failures reflect the poverty and relative instability of the two sets of economies as compared with the West,[17] some their relative newness and inexperience in the field, and some the pervasiveness of bureaucratic control that, for all its planning, and constant reorganization, seems fated to confound intention with performance at every turn.[18] Taken as a whole, however, these failures suggest simply that the South is unable to supply the items most wanted by the East in the quantity and of the quality required,

and that the East is under little pressure to help them do so. Far
from the two sets of partners being complementary to each other,
they suffer from a fundamental structural incompatibility.

In some sense, this has been recognized by Eastern economists.
They have almost always stressed the contingent and convergent nature
of East-South complementarity and the need to set about turning it
into an actual functioning relationship. They have called for structural
adjustments in their own economies to make a place for the South;
and for heavy investments in the South to help it claim that place.
What they have tended to avoid, at least in open debate, is discussion
of the full impact of such a program.

In both sets of countries the effects would go far beyond the
changes in economic policy and institutions already achieved. In
the East, the price and economic reforms on which meaningful integration of the South rests are themselves too tied to the diffusion of
economic and political power throughout the system to be undertaken
smoothly or fast or—if the retaking of Czechoslovakia in 1968 is any
guide—at all, without revolution. In the South the social and political
obstacles are, if anything, more daunting. The individual countries
are normally so badly integrated nationally, so inflexible economically,
and so open to outside influences that it would be no less revolutionary
to attain the minimum measure of control over domestic resources
that would make effective planning possible and with it active integration with the East.

Integration might be revolutionary, but it is not necessarily
unmanageable. It would be easier, of course, were the East able or
willing to finance it, to fund the oft-repeated commitment to "assist
in every way the development of the productive forces of the liberated
countries as the material basis for economic and social progress."[19]
But there is nothing to show that they are willing and able, or that
they might be. To the contrary, the amount of credit they have advanced
is small by any standard—Russia's annual commitments at the beginning
of the 1960's were of the order of 1.5 percent of gross fixed investment
and have fallen since. They have made it clear in innumerable ways
that resources for the South are limited; that they are "rendered not
from surpluses, but at the expense of diverting funds and materials
from what would be most useful to the socialist countries themselves";
that the East would not be blackmailed into credits, since "the socialist
countries have never entered into competition with capitalism in the
volume of the capital resources they export to the developing countries
and in the existing stage of development they cannot do so";[21] and that,
baldly, if the South needs or wants more they will have to find it in

the West: "A significant portion" of Asia, Africa and Latin America's requirements for capital, equipment, and technical assistance "needs to be satisfied through the agency of the imperialist states."[22]

At the same time a hardened commercialism has increasingly obtruded in the relations between the two sets of countries. As the South's dependence on Eastern markets grew so did the pressure on it to buy as a condition of further sales;[23] to reverse the favorable terms of trade that promoted the exchange in the first place;[24] to pay for know-how, which at first invariably came as a free gift;[25] and to pay very heavily for large numbers of narrowly qualified (European) experts.[26] Russia has made no concessions to Southern raw materials exporters in competition in the West, undercutting them in oil or tin, using their difficulties in the Middle East to break into their traditional markets.[27] Nor has Russia shielded them from its own difficulties: Together with the East European countries, they were made to share the whole burden of readjustment precipitated by Russia's balance-of-payments crisis in 1963-65, in order to safeguard Russia's trade with the West.[28]

Economic development in the South has not been given any sort of priority in the East: their economists have spent little time on it and concentrated almost exclusively on trade and marketing problems: Eastern countries have sold arms not given them[29] and so drained the South of development funds;[30] they have sold machinery and equipment without constructing self-sustaining industrial matrices linked to the recipient economies and without absorbing the surpluses that result.[31] Some Eastern countries have even claimed the right to bypass the state trading and other institutions set up especially for East-South trade.

Above all the East has shown no intention of bringing about the world-wide "stable distribution of labor" they promote in words: For every Algerian wine deal there are dozens of planning directives that, when implemented, would displace major Southern products from the import list. Russia and East Europe have already reduced purchases of natural rubber to make room for their growing synthetic rubber industry. Russia planned a 20-percent increase in natural cotton production and an immense increase in the output of synthetic fibers in the second half of the 1960's. Annexing Cuba to the South for a moment, domestic sugar production throughout the East grew despite the island's needs and representations. These three commodities accounted for half the East's imports from the South at the time the plans were formulated. In addition, Russia was aiming at self-sufficiency in tea by the end of the decade, and at a substantial rise in rice production, natural wool output, synthetic leather, ferrous and nonferrous metals—anything and everything it could conceivably produce at home. The point is not that the plans are always fulfilled but that they are intended to be. Their very formulation leaves little substance to dynamic complementarity as a goal.

The goal itself has been abandoned more or less.[32] Russia and the East European countries now openly tie their credits to export promotion projects as distinct from the import substitution policy that ruled in general up to 1965.[33] The exports in question are seen almost exclusively as primary products currently, or expected to be, in short supply—fuels, mineral ores, tropical foodstuffs. While obeisance is still made, albeit less frequently and less fulsomely, toward building industrial complexes that would permit the South to take an active and equal part in the "intrasectoral exchange" of dynamic complementarity, that is for the future. For the present and for the next ten to twenty or fifteen to twenty years, depending on the source, the exchange "will still be mainly of an intersectoral nature [the exchange of manufactures for agricultural commodities and minerals]."[34]

Whatever the immediate reasons for such a fundamental reversal of intentions, their effect is hardly likely to remain within the bounds of assimilating conventional Western views. As Russia and East Europe mature they can be expected to take on many of the economic behavior patterns of the West: a tendency to form closer economic links with developed countries East and West; a tendency to exclude the South from the major flows in trade, investment, and technology, and even as a supplier for some crude materials; and thence to a tendency to widen the gap between North and South in wealth, power, and in range of choice, whether economic or not.

These tendencies are clearly at work. Since the mid-1960's— earlier in some cases—East-West trade has diversified in scope and has become more flexible both conceptually and administratively. It is now no longer a pure exchange of products, but extends to the exchange of parts, processes, and services, through licensing (not all one way) and product-sharing arrangements, industrial cooperation agreements, and a network of new institutional instruments. These have been backed by ever-larger and longer-termed loans from the West and by specialization for Western markets in the East.[35]

On the other hand, the economically most advanced of the Eastern countries show the least interest in the South: East Germany has the lowest actual trade; and Czechoslovakia, the next in line, the sharpest declining trend. Romania, for whom geographical diversification in trade is <u>politically</u> important, nonetheless presents a forbidding prospect as a customer for any but the standard range of primary and traditional products;[36] and Poland, Hungary, and Yugoslavia, which share a relatively large stake in East-South trade allow nothing to cloud the essentials: It is a surrogate for the East-West trade they need but cannot always get.

None of this is fortuitous. Faced with the unremitting pressures of world-wide military and economic competition and the growing truculence and power of their own people, the Eastern bureaucracies simply cannot afford to forego the technical and organizational advantages of a Western-type economic maturity, no matter how insistent the lobbying from the South.*

The shift in the East's approach to the South has brought some notable ironies in its wake. One is the discovery of a problem celebrated in Western development literature as the problem of "limited absorptive capacity" or, in Russian, the "great difficulties caused by the extreme economic backwardness and limited financial and technical possibilities."[37] It is a problem that exists only in the context of social and political continuity in the recipient countries. For the East to recognize it, is of a piece with their policy of trying to secure that continuity by all political and military means; of a piece, too, with the revulsion of a section of the Southern middle class—"Maoists" here, "Guevarists" there, elsewhere something yet again—which is wholly committed to economic development as the basis for its rule and which cannot avoid seeing the East's slip from dynamic to static complementarily, from intra- to intersectoral exchange, as East-West complicity or worse.

Even more strange an irony is the East's conversion to the expensive pre-Stalinist orthodoxies of gradualism in economic development which it is, however, unwilling and probably unable to finance. Where the East relied on countervailance to win a place in the world economy for itself, the South is advised to try integration; where the East poured all its resources into broadbased industrialization and reduced to a shadow its points of direct contact with the outside world,

---

*Appendix B of this book reproduces a typical list of demands made of the East. It is part of the Charter of Algiers, adopted in October 1967 at the Ministerial Meeting of the "Group of 77," which formed at the UNCTAD meeting in 1964 in order to present a common Southern front to the wealthier countries.

the South is expected to concentrate on primary production, to open up its markets to world trade, to free such trade from administrative restrictions, and so on. The irony is the more acid in that even a Stalinist strategy, let alone a pre-Stalinist one, could probably not cope with the scale and complexity of effort required for development in today's unstable post-Stalinist world.*

If the trend toward a Western-type economic maturity persists in the East, which there seems no good reason to doubt, and if its consequences are not wholly at variance with what has been sketched here, it would be reasonable to draw two conclusions about East-South trade in general. One is that however large a volume it might attain in practice and notwithstanding its great importance to particular countries and particular trades, it will continue to be a residuum in intention, a consequence of both parties not finding adequate markets in the West, either because they are prevented from doing so or because they are unable to make the products and meet the standards required. Commitments will continue to be broken on both sides; and trade deficits run up as far as is possible within the bounds of bilateralism whenever prospects in the West improve. Each will continue to press for imports with a high convertible-currency content and withhold similar exports;[38] and each will try to interpose itself as an intermediary in the other's trade with the West. Since the Eastern economies are stronger, more developed, and maturing rapidl they are the more likely to succeed. For them East-South trade will become more of a residuum in fact as well as in intention, while for the South fact and intention will tend to diverge.

The second conclusion is that the phenomenal rates of growth achieved in the 1960's will tend to decline once the South's debt repayments converge on the East's reluctance to provide more and cheaper resources. As it is, debt service payments—estimated at $400 million in 1967 and rising fast—absorbed 18.3 percent of the South's exports to the East in that year;[39] and some of the major recipients of Eastern credit in the past—Indonesia, Ghana, India, Egypt have defaulted or come very near to doing so. Neither the burden of debt nor the difficulty of simultaneously expanding both trade and pay- ments is unlikely to ease in the near future.

To conclude and end near where this Introduction began, it can be said that the volume of East-South trade and its recent dynamism

---

*This line of thought is elaborated in Appendix A of this book.

indicate very little in themselves. They say nothing about causes
and prospects: whether growth reflects a long-term convergence of
interests between the two sets of countries or a transient conjunction.
To find that out it is necessary to reach behind the statistical aggre-
gates to their components—the major East-South trade flows—and,
within these, to the behavior and motivations of the traders and
trading organizations themselves.

That is what is attempted in the core of this study. Austerely
empirical throughout, it presents in Chapter 1 the pattern of trade
between Pakistan and the East as it formed during the 1960's,
disaggregated by partner (Russia, China, East Europe) and province
(East and West Pakistan); analyzes the effect on the statistical record
of switch-trading, which is widely practiced in East Europe, and of
other factors; and considers barter as an instrument of trade
promotion.

Chapter 2 assesses the importance for Pakistan (and for East
and West Pakistan separately) of the EBC's collectively and individu-
ally as markets and sources of supply for individual commodities; and
considers some of the biases in the statistical record. This is done
at a high level of product differentiation (4-digit level in the Pakistan
Standard Trade Classification [PSTC]).

Chapter 3 deals with the impact of EBC trade on the commodity structure of Pakistan's exports and develops a method of
measuring trade intentions.

In Chapter 4 prices of exports and imports to and from the
EBC's are compared with world prices and found to be significantly
and systematically different, for substantially "unpolitical" reasons.
The analysis is conducted at a PSTC 6-digit level and disaggregated
by partner and province.

Chapter 5 deals with some of the constraints on trade expansion
and concludes that Pakistan-EBC trade is unlikely to show as much
buoyancy in the future as it has in the past.

Since the study has generated a great deal of new data that
provide substance for a richer crop of observation and conclusion
than is gathered in its prose, text and tables have been more or less
segregated (text in Part I and tables in Part II of the book). Both are
meant to be read, for although they are closely related, they do
contain different sorts of information.

NOTES

1. It has been suggested that the EBC's, or Russia at any rate, artificially create deficits on their trading account with the South "as a means of obtaining economic entrée into a tight market clearly under the American sphere of influence" as in Latin America. See Marshall I. Goldman, Soviet Foreign Aid (New York: Praeger, 1967), p. 156. See also Carole A. Sawyer, Communist Trade with Developing Countries 1955-65 (New York: Praeger, 1966), p. 61, passim.

During the period in question, 1960-65, Russia's cumulative export surplus with thirty countries totalled $1.4 billion compared with a $1.1-billion cumulative import surplus with nineteen countries. See United Nations Conference on Trade and Development Secretariat, Review of Trade Relations among Countries Having Different Economic and Social Systems, Part II: Trade Between the Socialist and Developing Countries, (henceforth UNCTAD, Trade Between), TD/B/128/Add. 2, (Geneva: UNCTAD, July 21, 1967), Table 6, p. 12 (mimeo). Since then Russian economists have drawn attention to the damage caused to their own convertible currency reserves by the adverse trade balances with some Southern countries. See, for example, V. Savelyev, "Foreign Exchange Relations between Developing and Socialist Countries," Ekonomicheskiya Nauki, January 1968, quoted in Robert S. Jaster, "Foreign Aid and Economic Development: The Shifting Soviet View," International Affairs, 45, no. 3 (July 1969), 460.

2. See, for example, Economic Commission for Asia and the Far East (henceforth ECAFE) Secretariat, "Trade Between Developing ECAFE Countries and Centrally-Planned Economies," Part III (Case Studies) in Proceedings of the United Nations Conference on Trade and Development, (henceforth UNCTAD 64) Geneva, March 23,- June 16, 1964, Vol VII (New York: United Nations, 1964), p. 46 ff., in which Burma appears to be the only exception in a run of countries with very favorable terms of trade with the EBC's.

For India in the early days of trade with the EBC's, see Indian Institute of Foreign Trade (henceforth IIFT), India's Trade with East Europe (New Delhi: Ministry of Commerce, Directorate of Commercial Publicity, n.d. [1966]).

See also Raymond F. Mikesell and Jack N. Behrman, Financing Free World Trade with the Soviet Bloc, Princeton Studies in International Finance No. 8 (Princeton N.J.: Princeton University,

Department of Economics and Sociology, International Finance Section, 1958), pp. 73-74; Edith T. Penrose, The Large International Firm in Developing Countries: The international petroleum industry (London: Allen and Unwin, 1968), p. 194; Political and Economic Planning, East-West Trade (Planning, XXXI, no. 488) (London: PEP, May 1965), pp. 120, 130, and 143.

3. See, for example, UNCTAD, Trade Between, p. 39. Contrary complaints by interested parties in India have not been upheld (see ibid.; also IIFT, op. cit., pp. 28-30).

4. Vassil Vassilev, Policy in the Soviet Bloc on Aid to Developing Countries (Paris: Development Centre of the Organization for Economic Cooperation and Development, 1969), Tables 21 and 22, pp. 64-66.

5. Janusz Burakiewicz, "Some Problems in Trade Expansion with the Underdeveloped Countries of Asia, Africa and Latin America," Handel Zagraniczny, No. 6 (1962), pp. 245-46, quoted in Sawyer, op. cit., p. 79. See also Goldman, op. cit., p. 186.

6. It is given as 5.4 in Institute of Economics of the World Socialist System, Innovations in the Practice of Trade and Economic Cooperation between the Socialist Countries of Eastern Europe and Developing Countries (henceforth Institute of Economics, Innovations), a study presented to UNCTAD, Trade and Development Board, Ninth Session, Geneva, August 26, 1969, TD/B/238 (Geneva: UNCTAD, June 17, 1969), Table 5, p. 21 (mimeo). The aggregate coefficient given for East Europe and the South in the table is clearly a misprint and is corrected here.

7. Ibid., p. 23.

8. Russia's agreement to lift 10 million hectoliters of Algerian wine in 1969-70 is a recent dramatic example of its acting politically as a "buyer of last resort." The explanation for it is interesting and, given certain favorable and slightly outmoded assumptions about the nature of economic development, not far-fetched. The Institute of Economics writes about it:

> This agreement goes beyond the bounds of a purely commercial transaction: it will maintain business activity in a major sector of Algeria's economy which has been particularly badly hit by the unfavourable situation on foreign

markets. Algeria now has a stable wine market for many
years ahead and can take this into account in elaborating
development plans

which can be expected to lead ultimately to a reduction in Algeria's
dependence on wine exports. (Institute of Economics, Innovations,
p. 48).

9. This because apparent during their negotiations with the
newly independent East African states. See John Butler, The Soviet
Union, Eastern Europe and the World Food Markets (New York:
Praeger, for the Economist Intelligence Unit, 1964), p. 37.

10. S. Albinowski, A. Bodnar, S. Polaczek et al., cited approvingly
by Institute of Economics, Innovations, p. 86, passim; and ibid., Annex I.

11. See, for example, Lev L. Klochkovsky, Trade Prospects in
Socialist Countries. Union of Soviet Socialist Republics: Conditions,
Policies, Approaches, a study presented to UNCTAD, Trade and
Development Board, Tenth Session, Geneva, August 26, 1970, TD/B/
303 (Geneva: UNCTAD, June 26, 1970), p. 19 (mimeo.); L. Z. Zevin,
"Problems of Development of Export Oriented Industries in Developing Countries with Regard to the Expansion of Their Cooperation
with Socialist Countries," Summary of a note prepared for UNIDO,
reprinted in Private Enterprise in International Commerce, Selected
Papers from The National Conference held in Dacca, June 24-25,
1968, n.p. (Karachi: The Federation of Pakistan Chambers of Commerce and Industry in Association with (the) Pakistan Jute Association
and (the) Pakistan Jute Mills Association, n.d. [1968]) (not numbered
sequentially).

12. UNCTAD, Review of International Trade and Development
1969/70, Part One: Recent Trends in Trade and Development (henceforth UNCTAD, Recent Trends), TD/B/309 (Geneva: UNCTAD August
7, 1970), Table III-6, p. 38.

13. A brief presentation of the range of expectations at the
time may be found in an UNCTAD Secretariat paper, "Past Trade
Flows and Future Prospects for Trade between the Centrally-Planned
Economies and Developing Countries," in UNCTAD 64, Vol VI, pp.
170 ff., summarized on p. 224; achievements are taken from UNCTAD,
Recent Trends, Annex Table I. See also General Agreement on Tariffs
and Trade, International Trade 1969, (Geneva: GATT 1970), p. 136
where the shortfall is given as 40 percent.

14. From Stockholm International Peace Research Institute (SIPRI), Yearbook of World Armaments and Disarmament 1969-70, Table 1F.2, p. 341, crudely related to UNCTAD, Recent Trends, Annex Table I.

15. International Monetary Fund, Direction of Trade, relevant issues.

16. See, for example, Vassilev, op. cit., p. 51 ff.; Sawyer, op. cit., pp 64-65; UNCTAD, "Past Trade Flows," op. cit., Charts 1 and 2, pp 236-37; Mikesell and Behrman, op. cit., Table 10, p. 79; and Egon Neuberger, The European Soviet Bloc and the West as Markets for Primary Products: Stability, Growth and Size (Santa Monica, Calif.: The RAND Corporation, 1963), passim.

17. For the East see Frederic L. Pryor, Public Expenditures in Communist and Capitalist Nations (London: Allen and Unwin, 1968), pp. 296-99.

18. For a succinct description and analysis of the malfunctioning as it affects foreign trade see Alan A. Brown, "Towards a Theory of Centrally Planned Foreign Trade," in Allan A. Brown and Egon Neuberger, eds., International Trade and Central Planning (Berkeley and Los Angeles: University of California Press, 1968), pp. 60-61.

19. G. M. Prokhorov, Dve mirovyye sistemy iosvobodivshchiyesya strany (The Two World Systems and the Liberated Countries) (Moscow: Ekonomika, 1965), p. 205 quoted in David Morison, "USSR and Third World III. Questions of Economic Development," Mizan, December 1970, p. 135.

20. Pravda editorial, October 27, 1965.

21. S. I. Tyul'panov, Ocherki politicheskoy ekonomii: razviva-yushchiyesya strany (Essays in Political Economy: Developing Countries) (Moscow: Mysl,) p. 135.

22. V. Tyagunenko, "Aktual'nye voprosy nekapitalisticheskogo put razvitiya," Mirovaya Ekonomika i Mezhdunarodnye Otnosheniya [Current Problems in the Non-capitalist Path of Development, World Economy and International Relations] November 1964, p. 17.

23. At random-From Russia: "A corresponding increase of purchases of Soviet goods by developing countries is the main

prerequisite of our import's growth." N. S. Patolichev, U.S.S.R. Minister of Foreign Trade, quoted in Klochkovsky, op. cit., p. 37.

From Czechoslovakia: "The access to the Czechoslovak market for foreign goods may be expected to grow more or less in direct relation to the growth of Czechoslovak exports, which in turn depends on the effective access to foreign markets for Czechoslovak products." Miroslav Pravda, Vladimír Nováček, and Zdeněk Venera, Trade Prospects in Socialist Countries. Czechoslovakia: Conditions, Policies, Approaches, a study presented to UNCTAD, Trade and Development Board, Tenth Session, Geneva, August 26, 1970, TD/B/ 305 (Geneva: UNCTAD, June 17, 1970), p. 44 (mimeo.).

From Romania: "Increased imports of various products from developing countries have to be matched by a parallel increase in exports from Romania." Petre N. Popescu, Trade Prospects in Socialist Countries. Romania: Conditions, Policies, Approaches, a study presented to UNCTAD, Trade and Development Board, Tenth Session, Geneva, August 26, 1970, TD/B/304 (Geneva: UNCTAD, June 16, 1970), p. 32 (mimeo).

24. For reasons advanced in Chapter 4 below, and more fully by Baard Richard Stokke, in Soviet and Eastern European Trade and Aid in Africa (New York: Praeger, 1967), pp. 249-53, it is easier to defend the logic of this statement than offer quantitative proof, although the logic is supported by some very powerful assertions in China, Cuba, and, in its day, Yugoslavia, and by some evidence (as in Stokke).

25. Publicity literature still claims this to be true. See, for example, D. G. Chertkov, R. N. Andreyasyan, and YuI Mozhaev, SSSR i razvivayushchieyesya strany (The USSR and the Developing Coun- tries) (Moscow: Nauka, 1966), p. 36 passim, but it seems only applicable to market entry situations (see Vassilev, op. cit., p. 86).

26. Leo Tansky, "Soviet Foreign Aid to the Less Developed Countries," in U.S. Congress, Joint Economic Committee, New Direc- tions in the Soviet Economy (Washington: U.S. Government Printing Office, 1966), p. 961.

27. Robert E. Ebel, Communist Trade in Oil and Gas (New York: Praeger, 1970), p. 76.

28. Oleg Hoeffding, Recent Structural Changes and Balance of Payments Adjustments in Soviet Foreign Trade, (Santa Monica, Calif.: The RAND Corporation, May 1969), p. 15 passim (mimeo).

29. See Che Guevara on the absurdity of asking "of a people fighting for liberation, or needing arms to defend its freedom, whether or not they can guarantee payment." Che Guevara Speaks. Selected Speeches and Writings (New York: Merit Publishers, 1967), p. 114.

30. In the four years 1964-67, India's payments to Russia on defense account were expected to be 60 percent higher than payments on development loan account. Government of India, Ministry of Finance, Preliminary Memorandum on the Requirements of Assistance from the USSR for the Fourth Five Year Plan (New Delhi: n.p., May 1965), p. 77.

31. On India see Dietmar Rothermund, Indien und die Sowjetunion, (Tübingen: Böhlau Verlag, 1968), pp. 78-79; on Cuba see Guevara, op. cit., p. 110; and this despite highly publicized individual deals used to substantiate the claim that Eastern credit is self-liquidating.

32. The change was signalled in a series of articles in Voprosy Ekonomiki, beginning with G. Prokhorov's "Mirovaya sistema sotsial-izma; osvobodivshiyesya strany," No. 11, (1965) p. 82 ff.

33. There were exceptions, such as the agreement between Russia and Afghanistan in October 1963 for the repayment, in natural gas, of a 35-million ruble loan to set up an extraction and transmission system. This agreement seems to have acted as a pilot for the "production cooperation" arrangements made in the latter half of the decade, particularly in the "frontier economic complexes" such as Iran and Turkey. For a description of the Russo-Afghan agreement see David Morison, op. cit., p. 146.

34. Institute of Economics, Innovations, p. 33.

35. A useful base from which to monitor these developments is the Economic Bulletin for Europe's annual article on East-West trade: "Recent Developments in Trade Between Eastern and Western European Countries" (November 1967 and 1968) and "East-West European Trade . . ." No. 1, 1970 and No. 2, 1971). See also the UNCTAD Secretariat's summary annual Review of International Trade and Development; and Review of Trade Relations among Countries Having Different Economic and Social Systems.

For preliminary surveys of what might turn out to be a most significant integrative mechanism—the industrial cooperation agreement—see Michael Gamarnikow, "Industrial Cooperation: East Europe Looks West," Problems of Communism, May-June 1971;

and UNCTAD, Secretariat, <u>Industrial Cooperation in Trade Between Socialist Countries of Eastern Europe and Developed Market Economy Countries (including trade policy implications for the developing countries)</u> (Geneva: UNCTAD, June 19, 1969) (mimeo).

36. See Popescu, <u>op. cit.</u>, pp. 28-32.

37. B. Kozintsev, "Mezhdunarodno-pravovoe regulirovanie sotrudnichestva SSSR s razvivayushchimisya stranami" ("International Law Aspects of Soviet Collaboration with Developing Nations") in <u>Sovietskoye Gosudarstvo i Pravo</u>, No. 11 (1967), p. 126.

38. See below, p. 64.

39. From UNCTAD, Secretariat, <u>The Outflow of Financial Resources from Developing Countries</u>, TD/B/C./73 (Geneva, UNCTAD, February 20, 1970), p 17 (mimeo); and UNCTAD, <u>Recent Trends</u>, Annex I. Repayment of debt as a proportion of the South's exports to <u>Russia</u> are naturally very much higher. In 1964, when repayment of non-military loans accounted for 8 percent of exports to Russia and East Europe together, they were 20 percent of exports to Russia alone. Since disbursed loans on military account were by then larger than nonmilitary disbursements, the proportion of exports claimed by all loan servicing obligations was probably more than 40 percent (Sawyer, <u>op. cit.</u>, pp. 54-55) Vassilev, <u>op. cit.</u>, p. 68; Tansky, <u>op. cit.</u>, p. 957).

PART

I

AGGREGATE

Pakistan's trade with the Eastern Bloc Countries grew phenomenally during the 1960's—some five times in current values, or three times as fast as Pakistan's trade with the world as a whole (see Table II-1).

Not all the real growth has been recorded. The Central Statistical Office data on which this study rests exclude imports of "defense stores," which might have accounted for as much as $100 million a year and which appear to have switched from wholly Western to predominantly EBC suppliers over the decade.[1] The data exclude payment for services (other than insurance and freight on imports) that, in line with the growing range of products traded and the growing geographical diversification of trade, must be assumed to have increased faster than volume. And they suffer from other defects whose effects cannot be quantified even where their bias can be guessed at.[2]

But if all the real growth in trade has not been recorded, neither is all the recorded growth real. Although there has not been any discernible switch from trading through West Europe to trading direct, which might have artificially swelled the figures (what little use was made of intermediaries more or less ended, at least for jute, the major traded commodity of the time, by 1960,[3] there has been a rise in average import prices that if they kept step with prices of all imports over the decade, has more than offset a slight fall in export prices and might have accounted for some 12 percent of the recorded rise in trade.[4] And there has also been a certain amount of switch-trading, or diversion of cargoes from stated destinations.

25

This switch-trading is significant. Each consignment in or out of the country is covered by a shipping bill that records, among other things, its country of destination and its port of unloading. The two do not always correspond: Landlocked countries like Czechoslovakia or Hungary naturally need to use foreign ports for their sea-borne trade;* and maritime countries with infrequent or irregular direct cargo services to and from Pakistan find it convenient to use foreign ports for trans-shipping incoming and, to a less extent, outgoing freight.

Sometimes the lack of correspondence looks perverse, as when a cargoliner unloads goods in transit to one country at more than one trans-shipment port on one trip or, less significantly, when a plane unloads a cargo "in transit" at a foreign airport, for there is no financial or administrative rationale—nor has any been adduced in either Pakistan or EBC shipping or trading circles—for such costly duplication in handling charges.[5]

Multiple trans-shipment of this sort accounted for 23.5 percent of West Pakistan's stated exports to East Europe in 1969/70. Together with the small quantity sent by air to West European airports "in transit,"to Bulgaria in the main, 24.4 percent of West Pakistan's exports to East Europe through Karachi port and airport in that year were almost certainly intended not to arrive at their stated destination.[6]

Not all the East European countries switch-trade; and those that do, do so to very different degrees. Bulgaria, whose state trading organization (BULET) clearly engages in switch-trading professionally as the major normal, although unadmitted, part of its business, stands at one extreme with 72.9 percent. Yugoslavia, which appears to absorb all of its imports (as do Russia and China), is at the other extreme. In between lie Hungary (37.7 percent), Romania (32.6 percent), Czechoslovakia (23.3 percent) and Poland (4.8 percent) which use switch-trading both for normal commercial reasons and as a surrogate buffer-stock operation.[7]

If West Pakistan's exports are made to stand in for all Pakistan's exports in that year—not too solid an assumption since the bulkiness and easy identification of jute, East Pakistan's major export, make it a less—mobile commodity internationally than most of West

---

*Czechoslovakia has registered thirteen such ports with the Pakistan Customs; Hungary, twelve.

Pakistan's—and if it is further assumed, even less realistically,
that declared ports of discharge are always the actual ones,[8] at least
15 percent of Pakistan's ostensible exports to the EBC's as a whole
are currently finding their way directly to Western markets.[9]

Since switching is unlikely to have taken place at the volume,
and with the composition, of exports ruling in the early 1960's, it can
be held to account for something under 20 percent of the recorded
rise in exports to the EBC's or a little more than 9 percent of the
recorded increase in trade.

COUNTRY AND REGIONAL DISTRIBUTION

The very substantial rise in real trade that nonetheless took
place affected the trading partners and East and West Pakistan
unevenly. For the country as a whole, and excluding military supplies,
China proved the most sluggish partner and Russia the most lively
(slightly ahead of East Europe (see Table II-2).

The rise in trade with Russia was the most even-handed between
East and West Pakistan. With East Europe and China it was heavily
biased toward one or other of the two wings, China's trade with East
Pakistan rising on average at 2.3 times the West Pakistan rate, and
East Europe's trade with West Pakistan at 2.2 times the East Pakistan
rate (see Table II-2).

Relative weights changed sharply as a result: For East Europe
as a whole, East Pakistan was decisively replaced by West Pakistan
as the major trading partner, their relative shares in trade changing
from 2:1 in the first three years of the decade to 2:2.9 in the last
three. For China the reverse is true, the ratios having changed
from 2:2.2 to 2:1.3. Russia more or less perpetuated the initial
disparities. Seen from Dacca, China made substantial gains in share
of EBC trade from 22 to 37 percent between the first three and last
three years of the decade, largely at the expense of East Europe
(down from 61.8 to 46.3 percent), but also at the expense of Russia
(down from 16.7 to 14.5 percent). For West Pakistan the direction
of change was naturally symmetrical: East Europe up, from 39.7
to 53.0 percent, Russia up from 20.5 to 29.4 percent, and China down
from 39.6 to 17.3 percent (see Table II-1).

These changes depended on corresponding changes in the relative weights of exports and imports. Taking only the two trading
relationships that changed most significantly, East Pakistan's export

surplus with China dropped from 8.2 percent of trade turnover in the
first three years of the decade to 1.2 percent in the final three; while
West Pakistan's 31.8 percent import surplus with East Europe turned
into a 3.9 percent export surplus in the same period (from Table II-1).
In both cases a significant initial imbalance had more or less been
righted by the end of the decade.

THE INSTRUMENT OF GROWTH

The spurt in trade and the changes in its structure that occurred
in 1963/64-1966/67 (Table II-1) were closely linked to the barter,
or "commodity exchange" agreements that were concluded or pending
at the time.[10] These went beyond the terms that featured in the trade
pacts concluded immediately after World War II, [11] namely the granting
of most-favored nation treatment and indicating items of possible
trading interest. They set clear targets or ceilings for individual
items and stipulated that trade should balance, more or less, each
year. In this way they made it possible to replace settlement in convertible currencies with settlement through nonconvertible rupees
held in Pakistan, and so to insulate Pakistan-EBC trade to some extent
from world competition.

Barter deals quickly became typical of this trade, rising from
nothing to 66.3 percent of turnover in six years to 1968/69.[12] Where
no barter deals were concluded, trade stagnated at a low level as with
East Germany or Albania. Where they were concluded they were
carried to remarkable extremes. One Pakistan delegation found to
its embarrassment on visiting Romania when the provisions of the
then current Agreement were already realized, that

> the reception of the Romania side was extraordinarily
> cold. Not to speak of inviting the Mission to a reception
> or a dinner/lunch party, even the normal courtesy of
> providing transport was not extended. The Romanians were
> so indifferent to the Mission that they did not bother even
> guiding the Mission to their offices.[13]

An earlier trade mission, to Russia, found that an agreed export
quota for spectacle frames would not be taken up unless Pakistan
fulfilled its obligation to purchase medical equipment from the
importing agency; and that, further, the agency, Medexport, would
be willing to buy Pakistan surgical instruments only if Pakistan
would buy theirs.[14]

Although barter proper rapidly became the major vehicle for trade, it was not the only one. Credits, which were almost nonexistent before the flurry of trade agreements in the mid-1960's,[15] began thereafter to generate a fair volume of trade in their own right, and accounted for 44 percent of imports by 1968/69.[16] The distinction is not particularly meaningful however: Given that EBC loan and servicing repayments are in kind, credit agreements are best viewed as a form of long-term bilateral trading arrangement to be used when commercial exchanges are pressed beyond the limits of readily available commodities currently in surplus.

NOTES

1. Actual deliveries of U.S. military aid to Pakistan amounted to 97.1 million a year on average in the peak years 1958/60. Md. Abdus Scattar, United States Aid and Pakistan's Economic Development, unpublished Ph.D dissertation, Tufts University, 1969, Table II.3, p.47. Assuming military appetites to be no different from other institutional appetites (to grow with the eating and resist cutbacks); assuming too, that the switch from U.S. to EBC, mainly Chinese, sources entailed some movement away from low aid prices to quasi-commercial prices; and assuming that these prices reflect something of the price rise that has affected imports in general, 100 million a year seems low.

2. Tight control over foreign currency together with a highly overvalued exchange rate exert strong pulls to overreport and over-invoice imports and to underreport and invoice exports although the pull is less pronounced in trade with the EBC's. See Gordon Winston "Over-invoicing, Underutilization and Distorted Industrial Growth," Pakistan Development Review, Winter 1970, pp. 405-21.

In addition, until 1966/67 the central statistical office's (CSO) export figures included re-exports, normally no more than Rs (rupees) 2 million a year but liable to sudden fluctuations (as in 1967/68 when the ending of the Mangla Dam Project pushed the figure to Rs 22 million). This too was probably insignificant in EBC trade. Finally, changes in the trade classification used by the CSO (see CSO, Pakistan Standard Trade Classification Revised, June 1966) might have imported a bias, as might have the simple mistakes in recording and computation that abound in the published data.

3. China and, surprisingly, Russia have been buying their jute direct at least since 1951. The East European countries bought significant quantities through the West in the mid-and-late-1950's—7 percent of their requirements on average between 1955 and 1960, peaking in 1956 (15 percent) and 1957 (13 percent)—and have made few and small purchases since. See U. S., Department of Agriculture, World Trade in Selected Agricultural Commodities, 1951-65, Vol. 111: Textile Fibers, (Washington: U.S. Government Printing Office, 1968); U.S.S.R., Ministry of Foreign Trade, Vneshnyaya Torgovlya SSSR, relevant years, and Pakistan Central Statistical Office, Monthly Foreign Trade Statistics of Pakistan.

4. From Table II-1 rows 11 and 16. Average of 1960/61-1962/63 and 1967/68-1969/70. There is no satisfactory index for export and import unit values, hence no satisfactory index for Pakistan's terms of trade. The CSO's price indexes for raw materials and manufactures as given in the Monthly Statistical Bulletin recalculated with 1965/66 as a base, have been made to stand proxy for export and import deflators respectively and have been used to produce rows 15-19 in,Table II-1.

5. There is a small margin for error when a ship, say the Bliter loading in Karachi July 4-10, 1969, takes on a number of con-signments for a single country—Bulgaria in this case—to be discharged in three separate ports: Hamburg, Rotterdam, and Antwerp. One of the loads might be in transit to Bulgaria in fact. But there is no margin for error when a ship bound for the country's home port also discharges cargo "in transit" to that country in a foreign port: When, for example, the Nikola Tesla bound for Varna in Bulgaria, takes on cargo in Karachi, May 25-30, 1970, to be unloaded in Marseilles. Somewhere between these cases lies the single trans-shipment.

6. From the Karachi Customs House's Daily List of Exports and Imports for 1969/70, checked against the actual shipping bills for one month—May 1970. The Daily List, published by the Customs Houses at Karachi in West Pakistan, and Chittagong and Khulna in East Pakistan, tabulate the shipping bills. Since it proved impossible to find in Karachi any of the Daily Lists for Khulna, the main jute export port, nor a complete set for Chittagong, the analysis has been confined to exports from West Pakistan.

7. The criterion for switching as used in the text is probably too stringent for landlocked Hungary and Czechoslovakia. However there is no sensible way of adjusting their figures downward. The opposite is true in the Polish case. On a strict application of the criteria, Poland would seem to be switching no more than 3.9 percent of its imports from West Pakistan. However, a further 13.8 percent

was shipped via (single-) transit ports, which is a strangely high proportion on two counts. In the first place, the existence of a frequent, direct shipping service between Karachi and Poland's Baltic ports should make most trans-shipment redundant. Second, the ports that feature strongly as single-trans-shipment ports for certain commodities are also the major switch ports, and often the only offloading points for the same commodities; only one of twenty one consignments of hides and skins went direct (to Gdansk) while Hamburg alone took nine; Antwerp received all six consignments of crushed animal bones; and Zurich both shipments of sheep casings. By cautiously, enlarging the definition of switching to include trans-shipment of these three commodities, only the proportion of switched exports rises to the 4.8 percent adopted in the text.

8. It is naturally hard to pin down the evidence but exporters, shippers, and trade officials are free with anecdotes about ships outward bound from Karachi putting into Bombay for "repairs" and incidental unloading of their raw cotton cargo, or outward bound from Khulna putting into Calcutta with raw jute.

9. As long as their currencies are more overvalued in terms of convertible currency than the rupee, the East European countries will gain from this form of commodity arbitrage. During the first six months of 1970 the relevant average prices of the currencies in question were as follows:

Currency (1)	Effective Official Rate (2)	Free Rate (3)	Free Market Premium (3)/ (2) x 100
Ruble (Russia)	0.90	5.92	657.8
Zloty (Poland)	40.00 (T)	190.00	479.0
Koruna (Czech.)	16.20 (T)	45.00	277.8
Lev (Romania)	18.00 (T)	37.12	206.2
Forint (Hungary)	30.00 (T)	58.05	193.5
Lev (Bulgaria)	2.00 (T)	3.55	177.5
Diniar (Yugoslavia)	12.50	13.44	107.5
Mark (East Germany)	5.55	5.75	103.6
East Europe: arithmetic average free market premium 274.9			
Rupee (Pakistan)	4.76	10.75	225.8

Note: The tourist rate (T) has been used in preference to the lower official rate where choice exists. At basic official rates the average free market premium would be 550.

Source: Picks Currency Yearbook 1970.

10. In chronological order: Yugoslavia January 28, 1964; Hungary August 5, 1964; Bulgaria March 25, 1965; U.S.S.R. April 7, 1965; Poland December 10, 1965; Czechoslovakia January 29, 1966; China July 4, 1966; Romania July 7, 1966; and North Korea November 8, 1966.

11. Trade agreements were first signed with Czechoslovakia October 21, 1948; Yugoslavia April 1, 1949 (not ratified); Poland July 1, 1949; Hungary November 27, 1950. China came later, on March 14, 1953; and Russia—after an exploratory one-shot "Barter Agreement" in 1952—still later on September 3, 1956. This last agreement continues to provide the legal framework for U.S.S.R.-Pakistan trade.

12. Ministry of Commerce.

13. Unpublished Report of the Pakistan Trade Mission to Romania, Bulgaria, Yugoslavia and Albania (Karachi: Chamber of Commerce and Industry, November 1969) (typescript).

"The Mission," the Report continued sadly, "indirectly suggested to be taken out of Bucharest for an excursion on Sunday, November 16, 1969. The Romanian Chamber of Commerce bluntly informed the Mission to make their own arrangements. The Mission did undertake the trip on their own. The outing was quite interesting."

The story continues: "The Mission requested a meeting with the Romanian Minister for Foreign Trade with the excuse that the Leader of the Mission wanted to give him a personal present of Pakistan silver-ware. Even such a meeting could not be arranged."

It ends, however, on a note of defiance: "In view of the disappointing attitude of Romania, the Mission decided, in consultation with [the Second Secretary, Embassy of Pakistan, the Ambassador having 'gone out of Bucharest'] not to give the present."

It might be, as the Ministry of Commerce thinks, that some trade missions court this kind of treatment by their choice of members and their behavior on tour, but there seems little support for this view outside Islamabad. Both Pakistan and East European trading circles opted for the interpretation given in the text.

14. S. H. Akhtar, Report of the Pakistan Trade Delegation to U.S.S.R. Hungary and Poland from 8th April to 29th April 1967, n.p., n.d. (duplicated). The author, then Director, Export Promotion Bureau, acted as official adviser and secretary to the trade delegation.

15. Russia had granted a $30-million loan for oil exploration in March 1961, and Yugoslavia $6 million in export credits for the purchase of two ships (November 1962) and a slaughter house (April 1963).

16. Data Supplied by the Economic Affairs Division, Ministry of Finance.

2

IMPORTANCE
OF THE EBC'S
TO PAKISTAN

By the end of the 1960's the EBC's were accounting for slightly under 12.5 percent of Pakistan's foreign trade (Table II-1). They had become important for many crucial commodities and crucial for some, as can be seen from Tables II-3 to 6. They were even more important for East and West Pakistan considered separately; and some of them, of course, were more important than others (Tables II-7 to 14).

This importance is not altogether what it seems. As has been shown, East Europe is emerging as a trading intermediary with the West: Some 15 percent of exports to the EBC's is almost certainly switched to Western markets while en route. Another small, possibly very small, portion is re-exported after reaching its stated destination. Yet another portion is so closely bound up with East Europe's own export performance in the West as to constitute the substance of an implicit switching little different from the more open varieties.

Pure re-exports are very difficult to trace, partly because they consist largely of undifferentiated raw or processed materials that cannot be singled out in international trade statistics, partly because "there is no systematic machinery at the disposal of the Ministry of Commerce to follow up the movement of exports to detect cases of re-export,"[1] and partly because it is not always in the interests of the Ministry to reveal the instances that come to its notice.[2] Nonetheless, a few cases have been substantiated although not so many to upset the Ministry's conclusion that direct re-exports are probably unimportant, "far fewer than (is) usually made out."[3] And that is as it should be, for re-exporting is inherently costly and there are other methods of achieving the same results.

One method is implicit switching, whereby Pakistan goods are imported into the EBC's solely in order to free resources for their own export drive in Western Europe. It is almost impossible to trace. Unlike simple switching and re-exporting it breaks no agreements; and since it differs from international trade as normally understood only in denying domestic consumers the choice between home and Pakistan goods it is almost indistinguishable. Yet it fully explains the explosive increase, from nothing, to Rs 2.35 million, in sales of carpets and rugs (PSTC codes 6575 and 6576) to Romania in the last two years of the decade; it provides much of the steam behind repeated East European requests to lift restrictions on the export of cotton yarn; and some, at least, of the dynamism in their imports of grey cotton cloth (PSTC code 6521), up from nothing in 1965/66 to Rs. 57.71 million in 1969/70, or 10.6 percent of Pakistan's exports to the EBC's 17.8 percent of exports to East Europe, the key market, and 35.7 percent of total exports of that commodity.[4]

For these reasons alone the EBC's are less important as an export market than appears from the figures. At the same time, for reasons that do not emerge from the figures, they are a great deal more important than they seem as a source of supply—as providers of "military stores." But that is a closed book.

Some of the tables* suggest a "near-Cuban" shift in the direction of trade for some important commodities—the replacement of West by East. That it might also be near-Cuban in effect—a replacement of one dependency by another—derives from two interrelated circumstances of EBC trade. One is the consistency with which the EBC's assure themselves more than one source for each commodity, even within the narrow set of underdeveloped countries, so that Pakistan, despite her most strenuous efforts to ease out competitors[5] has never been the sole supplier, not even of jute and jute products.[6] The second is the ease and readiness with which EBC foreign trade organizations shunt bits of their rigid global import quotas for individual commodities between countries and currencies in response to price and other incentives.[7]

With this said, Pakistan has succeeded in finding a new and important market in the EBC's. They accounted for 25 percent of the increase in trade over the decade. Their share of turnover trebled, and Pakistan's dependence on a small set of Western trading partners

_____

*See Tables II-5, 6, 9, 10, 13, and 14.

declined.[8] In terms of its stated trade objectives, namely the "diversification and expansion of exports" and the "diversification of the sources of imports,"[9] the Government of Pakistan can claim to have had something of a success.

NOTES

1. Ministry of Commerce, Review of Pakistan's Trade with East Europe, July 1964-June 1969 (henceforth Ministry of Commerce, Review) (Islamabad, 1970), p. 11.

2. The Government of Pakistan has often winked at East European purchases for third parties when the commodities in question were in surplus, for example: raw cotton—a deteriorating commodity—in 1967/68; chrome ore to Canada via Poland in 1968; jute and jute products to Western Europe via Bulgaria, constantly.

3. Ministry of Commerce, Review, p. 12.

4. CSO and interviews with East European trade representatives.

5. Pakistan trade officials spend a great deal of energy in trying to encroach on India's share of the EBC market, and have made bids even for Thailand's miniscule share of the jute and jute-equivalent (kenaf) market in the EBC's. For the latter see S. H. Akhtar, Report of the Pakistan Trade Delegation to U.S.S.R., Hungary and Poland from 8th April to 29th April 1967, n.p., n.d. (duplicated), pp. 24, 33.

6. See, for example, Lev L. Klochkovsky, Trade Prospects in Socialist Countries. Union of Soviet Socialist Republics: Conditions, Policies, Approaches, Annex II: "The geographical distribution of the U.S.S.R.'s imports from the developing countries." Miroslav Pravda, Vladimír Nováček and Zdeněk Venera, Trade Prospects in Socialist Countries: Czechoslovakia: Conditions, Policies, Approaches, Annex VIII: "Source of supply of a number of products of interest to the developing countries"; and Petre N. Popescu, Trade Prospects in Socialist Countries: Romania: Conditions, Policies, Approaches, Annex VII: "Sources of imports into Romania of products of export interest to developing countries 1968," all, studies presented to UNCTAD, Trade and Development Board, Tenth Session, Geneva, August 26, 1970, TD/B/303, 305, 304 (Geneva: UNCTAD, June 26, June 17, and June 16, 1970) (mimeo).

7. Or, as Klochkovsky puts it,

the state of the balance of payments . . . exerts a very
considerable influence on the volume of exports and
imports of individual goods envisaged by the draft plan,
both for trade with groups of countries and especially for
trade with individual countries. In this connexion, and
also because of fluctuating market conditions during the
period of the plan, the actual results of trade in respect of
particular countries may vary substantially from the ini-
tially planned figures. By allowing for these fluctuations
in their operations with individual countries, however, the
foreign trade organizations strive for the overall volume
of imports and exports to accord with the assignments of
the plan.

Klochkovsky op. cit., p. 55.

8. Joseph Stern's conclusion (in "A Note on the Structure of
Foreign Trade," Pakistan Development Review, Summer 1969, pp.
219-20) that "the percentage share of exports purchased by . . . ('the
Afro-Asian region and the Socialist Bloc') did not show any upward
trend" between 1960/61 and 1967/68 reflects inter alia the sudden dip
in trade following the Suez Canal closure in the terminal year.

9. Ministry of Commerce, Review, p. 2.

3

STRUCTURE
OF
EXPORTS

The attempt to change the structure of Pakistan's exports via EBC trade has been less successful. Expectations were high from the beginning: "Pakistan's main interest in bilateral trade arrangements," went a typical review, "has been to sell manufactured goods instead of purely primary commodities."[1] And some official comments make it appear as if the expectations have been fulfilled, resoundingly. Thus, A. E. Erokhin, Trade Representative of the U.S.S.R. in Pakistan: "The share of manufactured and non-traditional goods in exports from Pakistan in 1970 has been raised to about 60 percent."[2] But success has had more to do with a complaisant nomenclature than with real values.

The Ministry of Commerce lists exports to the EBC's under two heads, "traditional" (Group I) and "nontraditional" (Group II) and sets a target ratio between them. The ratio itself has changed over the years from 50:50 in the mid-1960's to 60:40 or more now in favor of "nontraditional" items. But the composition of the two categories raises more questions than it answers: Group II contains nontraditional items only in the restricted sense that they are new as exports. They are not new, in a sense more relevant to development and to the government's own aims, in containing an exceptionally large skill or value-added content, or even that they are manufactures. Thus, to take a few examples at random, the 1967 trade agreement with Hungary, and the 1968/69 agreements with Poland and Czechoslovakia all included sheep-casing, animal hair, fish meal, crushed bones and bone meal, medicinal herbs, ores, and minerals with the more traditional "non-traditional" items listed as Group II exports.[3]

Reordering the data, even crudely as in Table II-15 leads to a very different outcome. Apart from a few minor quirks affecting five of the 150 observations in Section 1 of the table,* the EBC's and each component of the EBC's appear to have bought a far narrower range of commodities from Pakistan than has the world, measured by either of two dispersal indexes: the proportion of exports formed by the top three commodities (Section 2 of the table), or the number of significant traded commodities (Section 1). Their rate of "deconcentration" has been more or less the same as the world rate when measured by the first index, but rather faster when measured by the second (and would have been even faster were it not for the conservative behavior of the figures for trade with China). But not too much should be read into this result since it is implicit in the extreme commodity concentration with which exports to the EBC's began the decade.

Section 3 of Table II-15 shows an impressive, across-the-board growth in manufactured exports,** the linchpin of the government's foreign trade policy, with Russia well ahead and China trailing. Yet even here the impression derives more from the low initial starting level of exports than from anything more fundamental: On average, manufactures other than cotton textiles and jute goods performed less than 33 percent as well as all goods in reaching the bilateral export targets to East Europe and Russia, 1965/66-1968/69.[4]

The figures for trade with Russia are particularly detailed and therefore interesting. Exports of manufactures were very unstable in composition and volume in the first half of the decade, more unstable than all exports to Russia. But from 1965/66 the volume rose very rapidly, from virtually nothing in 1964/65 to Rs 12.6 million in 1969/70. Expansion was based on three commodities—footwear, clothing, and spectacle frames—which together provide more than 90 percent of total manufactured exports. The quantities are still to small and the experience of trade too short to sustain hard conclusions, but a first

---

*These result from the fineness of the commodity classification used, which lists bleached cotton yarn (PSTC 6513) for example separately from unbleached (PSTC 6514), or optical elements (8611) separately from spectacles and spectacle frames (8612).

**PSTC Section 8 commodities do not cover all manufactures. However, they include the nontraditional "miscellaneous manufactures" whose export would indicate best the degree to which official trade and economic policy objectives were being attained.

tentative exercise suggests that the thrust behind the export of manufactures is fairly weak.

Most trade between the two countries is governed by triennial
Agreements on (the) Exchange of Goods, which indicate annual targets
for each commodity. These are then amended or confirmed during
negotiations on annual trade plans.[5] Almost all other trade comes
under ad hoc commodity barter deals.[6] Ideally, were Russia intending
to meet Pakistan's stated trade objectives in fact and assuming away
all difficulties of supply, projected exports of manufactures would grow
faster than projected exports of processed goods from one three-years
agreement to the next, and projected exports of processed goods should
in turn grow faster than projected exports of raw materials. Using the
symbols explained in Chart I-1, the outcome would be $\Delta P^r < \Delta P^p < P^m$.

At the same time, export targets written into the annually negoti-
ated trade plan would come closer to the original projections or would
be more likely to exceed them the greater their manufactured content,
that is $\dfrac{Q^r}{P^r} < \dfrac{Q^p}{P^p} < \dfrac{Q^m}{P^m}$. The out-turn, or actual trade, would
show the disparity in target fulfilment even more sharply: $\dfrac{O^r}{P^r} < \dfrac{O^p}{P^p} < \dfrac{O^m}{P^m}$.

This interplay of the different degrees of manufactured intensity
with the different stages of the negotiating cycle should produce a
matrix for each year as explained in Chart I-1.

In fact, the relationships have turned out to be very different.
Table I-1 summarizes the relevant data from the trade agreements
and their amendments and from the Ministry of Commerce's internal
Implementation Reports. The results are instructive: In no year was
there full correspondence between expectation as set out in Chart I-1
and performance. For the period as a whole the incidence of correspondence was only slightly higher than the incidence of divergence, in the
ratio of 3:2 (see Chart I-2) and would have been lower but for the iden-
tities between projected and annual targets for the three Rice Barter
Deals and for the two years in which the triennial trade agreements
were signed, 1965 and 1968. Attaching values to the incidence of correspondence as is done in Chart I-3 shows performance to have been
contrary to expectations in all but three of the relationships. And
these three—to do with the very strong upward thrust in manufactured

TABLE I-1

Year-by-Year Percentage Change in Pakistan's Barter Exports to Russia, 1965-70
(Initial Projections, Annual Plans and Out-turn by Intensity of Manufacture)

	ΔP^r	ΔQ^r	ΔO^r	ΔP^p	ΔQ^p	ΔO^p	ΔP^m	ΔQ^m	ΔO^m	$\Delta\Sigma P$	$\Delta\Sigma Q$	$\Delta\Sigma O$
1965	+348.4	+387.4	+368.5	+47.8	-2.2	+26.1	+3.3	+162.2	+475.0	+244.0	+264.1	+312.1
1966	-18.3	-30.0	-19.4	+43.6	+168.2	+155.2	+41.7	+65.3	+352.2	-9.6	-9.9	-2.8
1967	-29.8	-16.6	-24.1	+46.6	+22.9	-22.3	+90.6	+16.9	-52.9	-8.7	-9.4	-26.6
1968	-24.0	-29.9	-34.4	+7.9	+7.9	+84.3	+12.3	-15.4	-14.3	-1.6	-14.4	-16.1
1969	+14.9	+49.8	—	+14.8	-8.7	—	+17.0	+26.2	—	+15.2	+27.2	—
1970												

Notes: Symbols as in Chart 1.

Source: Ministry of Commerce.

CHART I-1

Pakistan-Russian Trade: Anticipated Relationships
Between Targets Set and Hit at Different Stages
in the Negotiating Cycle and Products of different Degrees of Manufacturing Intensity

$$
\begin{array}{ccccc}
\Delta P^r & > & \Delta Q^r & > & \Delta O^r \\
\wedge & & \wedge & & \wedge \\
\Delta P^p & \leq & \Delta Q^p & \leq & \Delta O^p \\
\wedge & & \wedge & & \wedge \\
\Delta P^m & < & \Delta Q^m & < & \Delta O^m
\end{array}
$$

where: P = agreed initial projections written into
the three-year agreement
Q = annual trade plan targets
O = out-turn, or actual trade
r = raw materials (PSTC Sections 0-2)
p = processed products or very unsophisticated manufactures (PSTC Section 6)
m = manufactures (PSTC Section 8)
Δ = proportionate positive change

exports—are not too significant, since those exports started from
virtually nil in the period under review. Allowing for this and for its
decreasing effect as total volume rises, manufacturing exports can be
expected to converge on the underlying pattern shown in Chart I-3, a
pattern of buoyancy declining with manufacturing intensity and with
progress through the negotiating cycle.

The evidence is admittedly shaky, almost as shaky as the assumption that supply is elastic. It is even shakier for the rest of the EBC's
whose record of trade is generally shorter and statistically less
illuminated than is Russia's. Nonetheless it points—as does the more
circumstantial reasoning of Chapter 5—in a direction contrary to that
of most official spokesmen: The directions taken by geographical
and product diversification have not coincided in EBC trade and are
unlikely to.

CHART I-2

Pakistan Exports to Russia, 1965-70: Incidence of
Correspondence (+) and Divergence (-) between
Actual and Anticipated Quantitative
Relationships as Set Out in
Table I-1 and Chart I-1

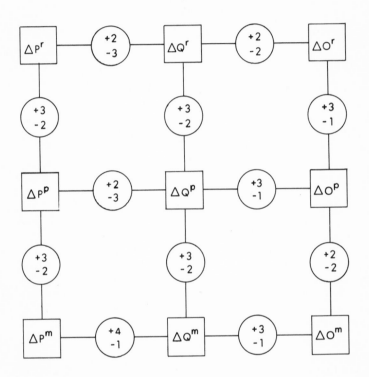

<u>Source</u>: Ministry of Commerce.

<u>Note</u>: Symbols as in Chart 1.

CHART I-3

Pakistan Exports to Russia, 1965-70: Average
Annual Percentage Divergence from (-)
or Correspondence with (+) Minimum
Norms of Anticipated
Relationships as Set
Out in Chart I-1

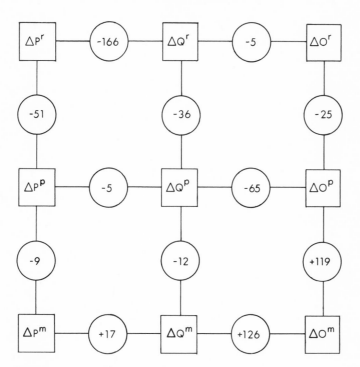

Source: Ministry of Commerce.

Note: Symbols as in Chart 1.

NOTES

1. Trade and Industry, July 1967, p. 1033.

2. "Pakistan-U.S.S.R. Trade Relations, Consolidated Barter
Agreement Mutually Advantageous," Pakistan Economist, IX, no. 3
(March 1970). 62.

3. From Schedule A of the relevant trade protocols. The Ministry
of Commerce is not alone in classifying exports by temporal rather
than qualitative newness, or in simply lumping incompatible products
into single categories. In private sector publications, Basmati rice
appears among more orthodox items, like jute manufactures or shoes,
as a new purchase of manufactures by Russia, (See for example, "Brief
Survey of (the) Russian Market," Trade and Industry, XI, no. 1
(January 1967), 228; S.H? Akhtar, Report of the Pakistan Trade Delegation to U.S.S.R. Hungary and Poland from 8th April to 29th April 1967
n.p., n.d. (duplicated), p. 11). From the other side, a Russian analyst
at the Scientific Research Institute of the Ministry of Foreign Trade,
classes "artifacts . . . wines, cognacs, grape alcohol" among his
country's "purchases of manufactures and semi-manufactures."
Lev L. Klochkovsky, Trade Prospects in Socialist Countries. Union
of Soviet Socialist Republics: Conditions, Policies, Approaches, a
study presented to UNCTAD, Trade and Development Board, Tenth
Session, Geneva, August 26, 1970, TD/B/303 (Geneva: UNCTAD, June
20 1970), p.20 (mimeo).

4. From Ministry of Commerce, Review of Pakistan's Trade
with East Europe, July 1964-June 1969 (Islamabad, 1970, Annex VIII,
p. 20.

5. There have been two such Agreement since the mid-1960's,
dated April 7, 1965 and February 28, 1968. Subsequent amendment
is confirmed by the exchange of a letter following negotiation.

6. Since the mid-1960's there have been three Rice Barter
Deals, dated January 18, 1966, February 8, 1967, and May 9, 1968.

CHAPTER

4

PRICES

EXPORTS

Except for the one year 1965/66, prices obtained from the EBC's have been higher than world prices, the (weighted average) premium ranging from 102.9 percent in a bad year like 1963/64 to 136.9 percent in a good one like 1962/63.* For the decade as a whole the (weighted) average export price premium was 110.6 percent (from Table II-16). Sometimes, particularly for new exports, the disparity has been very large as can be seen from the detail of Tables II-17 to 26. Sometimes it has been less, but the tendency has been sufficiently marked and sufficiently consistent to need explaining.

On the whole the price premium is not intended. As an important part of the world market yet without a compatible pricing system, the EBC's central guiding principle in international trade can only be to buy (and sell) at what seems to be ruling world prices. Their foreign trade officials are under instructions to do so and clearly try to. By all accounts, they drive as hard and as unsentimental a bargain as anyone else under the same constraints; they speculate on major price movements like anyone else, witholding from bear markets as in raw jute early in 1969, or riding with the bulls as in raw cotton in 1968/69;[1] they take price advantage where they can, as in their

---

*No breakdown of export or import unit values by country or trading area exists for Pakistan. Unit value indexes exist, but they date from 1960/61 and do not account for the large increase in the number of traded commodities.

dealings with the Trading Corporation of Pakistan (TCP);[2] and they
are obviously pained and embarrassed at any suggestion that they
might not be behaving like economic men. And yet they pay above the
odds.

One reason is that much of the EBC's processing equipment is
relatively unsophisticated and requires a better-than-average quality
of raw material to achieve average quality output. This is readily
admitted in the case of the Polish and Czechoslovak jute manufacturing
industries, less readily in that of cotton textiles, and results in their
buying systematically at the top end of the market. Such fine distinc-
tions in quality are lost in the record even at the 6-and 7-digit level
of disaggregation used in Tables II-17 to 26 and so tend to exaggerate
the price premium paid.

But this can contribute only a small part of the explanation.
An analysis of raw jute sales for 1969/70, conducted especially for
this study by the Jute Trading Corporation, a major government
supply agency, shows that Poland paid between 4 and 10 percent more
on average, Czechoslovakia between 4 and 7.5 percent more than
West European buyers for the same quality of product (See Table II-
27). And this is in spite of the fact that both countries scrupulously
avoided paying more than the official minimum export price—the
"EPC price" set daily by the Export Price Committee—and that
Poland at least, kept a foreign trade official permanently in Dacca to
deal in jute and to follow market trends.

How does this come about? Since jute exports are among the
best recorded and controlled, since they are also the longest standing
from the EBC's point of view and therefore the trade in which they
are least likely to make mistakes through ignorance, it is as well to
pursue the explanation in this market. A Western jute buyer normally
has more information than his Eastern Bloc counterpart. It is not
a question of block-learning, or of studying seasonal price variations
in the past or of analyzing crop reports—in formal erudition the
Eastern Bloc buyer might well have the edge—but of receiving a
constant bombardment of fact and rumor that allows him to buy with
a degree of informed speculation, to "buy with a view" as it is known
in the trade. EBC traders do not have the personal network of
acquaintances, if not friends, or the common language and partially
shared experience that Western traders have. They are still relatively
small buyers, without, moreover, that most seductive of influences—
a pocketbook of convertible currencies. Except for the Bulgarians,
perhaps they cannot compete in providing channels for capital flight
or in the supply of sophisticated consumer durables; or even in the

provision of less durable, less sophisticated consumption abroad.[3]
And even the Bulgarians are scarcely in a position to act as a physical
sanctuary if normal commercial risk should escalate into risks for
commerce as such. Therefore they have to pay to exercise the
options opened up by the bilateral trade agreements—through the
premium in Pakistan export prices.

The EBC buyer is also hampered by his organization whose
rules and performance indicators normally leave little room for
profit-motivated behavior. These make life easier for the man who
sticks fast to the EPC prices, even at their peak, than for the man
who buys forward at a lower price but one that happens to be above
EPC on that day. The result is that the Eastern Bloc buyer is relatively
insensitive to the maneuvers and even to the motives behind them
that edge him from the troughs toward peak EPC prices even during
the jute delivery months when prices are at their year's ebb.

Neither is he helped by the marked uneveness in the flow of
goods and payments between the barter-trade partners. Some of
this is inherent in the asymmetry of the trade itself. Imports into
Pakistan are often large, complex, and costly, requiring a great deal
of supporting investment. Once ordered their schedules are difficult
to control, and once delivered, payments are lumpy. The result is
that exchanges of goods tend to outrun the periods for which they are
planned, and rupee balances undergo explosive build-ups after weeks
or even months of steady decline.[4]

But not all the unevenness in purchases and payments is inherent
in the trade itself. Some of it results from the behavior of the EBC
foreign trade organizations themselves—their attempt to offset the
fluctuations in rupee receipts by inducing a compensatory and wholly
artificial unevenness in purchases and payments for exports, with
little reference to seasonal and other factors that might affect local
prices. Add to this the special pressures generated toward the end
of a trade agreement to achieve balance at almost any cost and one
can begin to see the reasons for the typical price myopia of EBC
trade officials and understand the logic behind their "I have rupees"
or "I don't have rupees"—typical responses to queries about their price
behavior.

Unevenness in trade is inherent in the EBC-type economy in a
more general sense: They are relatively small traders and are
undercapitalized; they keep stocks to a minimum and shift stockholding
outside the system wherever and whenever possible. As a consequence
changes in production in one or two factories are as likely to result

in purchasing agents receiving new instructions—the example of jute
for Romania was quoted in support—as to changes in the level of
stocks held at home. There is little room left in which to exercise
commercial discretion on the spot.

Bilateralism does more than structure trade officials' responses
to price stimuli. It turns the trading partners into mutually tied
sources, that could, if they wished, bid up their supply prices above
world levels. Whether they all do so or not is a different matter.
Exporters of footwear and spectacle frames certainly do, the latter
by 5 percent or so, the former by more, and exporters of textiles
seem to, although to less extent. On their own admission the exporters
are satisfied with the present system. It allows them to remind
their EBC customers of their treaty obligations when prices are at
issue, and to call in the Ministry of Commerce if the customers
continue to balk. Given the size of orders, the small number of
possible suppliers who, moreover, know one another and act in concert,
and the inflexible rhythm of bilateral trading, there is little the EBC
partner can do in the short run but pay up (and dream aloud as the
Romanians and Hungarians, at least, have done, about the attractions
of free trade).

It would be wrong to end this section without reference to the
small micropolitical element in export pricing, which brings the
Chinese, and perhaps some of the other EBC's as well (although there
is no evidence one way or the other in their case) to favor certain
export houses over others and to tolerate somewhat idiosyncratic
prices. But it would be even more wrong to suppose this to be of
much significance. The most diligent inquiry threw up no more than
one probable case out of three possible ones.

By and large the EBC's do pay higher-than-world prices for
their purchases in Pakistan. They do so for a number of easily
identifiable reasons that can be read from the structure and organization of their own economies, from their relative weakness vis-à-
vis major Western competitors and from the nature of bilateral
trade. Politics, other than the macropolitics that led to the concluding
of bilateral trading agreements in the first place, hardly enters into
it.

IMPORTS

There is no joy in higher prices for exports that are fully
cancelled out by higher prices for imports. This has occurred in

intra-EBC trade[5] and might easily have occurred in EBC-Pakistan trade. But it seems not to have done so.*

Since government is the major current target for EBC sales, and machinery their major selling item, relative prices paid by state agencies for machinery should indicate and systematic bias that might exist. Three such comparisons were made for this study: of power transformers and electrical substations bought by the Water and Power Development Authority, and of textile spinning machinery as evaluated by the Industrial Development Bank of Pakistan (IDBP). In each case care was taken to compare like with like so that differences in quality or financial arrangements did not distort the results too badly.

Tables II-28, 29, and 30 summarize the results. They show an average East European price 25 percent below the West European average for power transformers, 17 percent below for substations, and a Russian price for spinning machinery 67 percent of the lowest Western offer and not much more than 50 percent of the highest. In no case did the East European price range overlap the higher West European one.

Not all the evidence is as clear-out. Sometimes it simply does not exist. The Russians at least find it unnecessary or impossible to break down their all-in price for a plant or a set of machines into its components, and would-be purchasers from Pakistan have been frustrated at every turn in trying to get them do so.[6] Even where prices do exist comparison is scarcely easy: With few exceptions it is distorted by differences in quality that are as difficult to assess in the absence of a freely competitive market as they are important to the final outcome.

For what such impressions are worth, most users of EBC machinery consider its technical performance satisfactory in most, not all, cases, and its economic performance poor. In the oil industry,

---

*This conclusion is far less solidly based than in the case of export prices. It has proved impossible either to construct a series of import unit prices out of published central statistical office (CSO) data, or—in the time available—to process the raw data available to the CSO. There are, however, enough scraps of evidence from which to form an impression, and which can be fed into a set of presumptions deprived deductively.

Russian equipment was reported to be "serviceable" but "below U.S. standards over the whole range," and the Oil and Gas Development Corporation has had to buy gravimeters and other specialized equipment from the U.S.[7] EBC metal-working machinery seems little better, ten-year old U.S. surface grinders and milling machines working to finer tolerances than their Russian or Chinese equivalents,[8] Russian printing machinery was found to be efficient, simple, and suitable to Pakistan conditions but dated.[9] In the all-important textile industry, Russian machinery was thought to be good to excellent, always robust and reliable and sometimes equal to the best anywhere, but with relatively high running costs. To quote the early report already cited, it is "steady, durable and may render about twenty years' satisfactory service even if run on three shifts. In performance they (sic) can be favourably compared with textile machinery of similar type and value, i.e. Japanese. The textile machinery of U.S.S.R. origin, however do not seem to be high production machinery."[10] However, Polish machinery—for textiles, ceramic products, dyestuffs, glassware, steel castings—seemed excellent technically, "better than some West European manufactures" in some instances, and with similar economic performance; as did some Czechoslovak and Yugoslav machinery.[11]

No matter how opinions on quality differ, in one respect there is near unanimity: The EBC's in general and Russia in particular are unable to offer adequate back-up facilities. Inattention to servicing and stockholding has, in cases shown to the author, resulted in one line of metal-working machines standing idle for two years for want of a few tools, and in another being immobilized for five years for want of a relatively small balancing item. They are unwilling to deal in small quantities, whether in setting up textile plants—"nothing less than a quarter of a million spindles"—or supplying sets of machine tools—not less than one hundred when a dozen were wanted. They seem ignorant of, or unwilling to adapt to, local conditions that results in Volga cars in West Pakistan being fitted with heaters, not air conditioners,* and in Russian motor cycles in East Pakistan

---

*Conversation in a Karachi showroom:
"Why heaters?"
"They have snow in Murree." (In the mountains northeast of Rawcelpiudi.)
"Do they have Volgas?"
"No. There are no servicing facilities."
"Do you plan to set them up?"
"No."

seizing up within a mild of starting for want of tropicalization.* Their procedures are labored and time consuming and their delivery lags both huge and unpredictable.

Such unanimity does not stretch far however. Even after accounting for quality and servicing, there is nothing approaching consensus on machinery prices. Even closely involved professional observers have not been able to reach a firm personal conclusion. Thus, Yusuf H. Shirazi, president of the Karachi Chamber of Commerce, was clearly impressed by price discounts in 1966: "Prices remain normal" under EBC long-term credit for machinery imports "as against heavy price increases when such arrangements are entered into with the Western powers."[12] By 1969, he had drawn back a bit: "Prices of some of the commodities imported from countries with whom Pakistan had barter agreements are competitive in the beginning but are scaled up afterwards, and this tendency is hampering the flow of barter imports."[13] But by the following year, in conversation with the author, he had come around again, albeit with reservations: Eastern Bloc machinery was cheap, but spares were expensive, sometimes outrageously, and frequently superseded by new, incompatible models. All in all, and despite much evidence to the contrary, the EBC machinery prices do seem cheaper than world prices for comparable items cheaper than might be justified by differences in quality or in servicing.

The same does not seem to be true of imported raw materials. Again, there are no decently aggregated figures to support a firm statement, but an analysis of zinc imports through the Trading Corporation of Pakistan suggests that EBC prices (c.i.f. Pakistan) have been 10.9 percent above world cash prices in the last three years of the period, higher even than Western tied-aid prices (Table II-31.**

---

*On the other hand, WAPDA officials are full of praise for the flexibility shown by EBC electrical machinery makers and their willingness to adapt their products to Pakistan usage (within the general framework of agreed international standards).

**There is of course the danger that a single commodity's price, particularly when imported by the TCP, might be unrepresentative, but without quantity data for raw material imports no general analysis can be attempted.

These results are no more than one would expect on general grounds. Almost all of the EBC's have undergone a very rapid, extensive, and, in principle at least, autarkic process of industrialization. They suffer, more or less acutely, from a shortage of raw materials both for their own use and as an earner of convertible currencies; and most enjoy a relative abundance of unsophisticated plant and machinery. In trade among themselves a two-tier market has developed in which raw materials are classed as "hard" goods and standard machines "soft." Naturally the same distinction appears in their trade with Pakistan. Their export schedules normally distinguish between the two classes of goods as do Pakistan's. So do their negotiating and commercial behavior. They are notably reluctant to part with raw materials, which results in delays and higher prices;* while their eagerness to pump plant and machinery into Pakistan is marked not only by a furious competition inter se in credit terms, occasionally free technology, high sales commissions and such, but also by their depressed market-entry prices.

PRICE MOVEMENTS

It seems reasonable to suppose that once inside the Pakistan market the EBC's would try to reverse the unfavorable terms of trade on which they gained entry. Businessmen generally believe this to be true.[14] Some know it to be true, notably the footwear manufacturers exporting to Russia who claim to have experienced a sharp pincer movement on quality and price in the last two years. On the other hand, major purchasers of heavy machinery, like the Water and Power Development Authority, have experienced no upward movement, and the government has found it possible to force down prices when they appeared out of line internationally.[15]

However, nothing conclusive can be said in the absence of unit value indexes for imports and exports.

---

*Where the EBC's arrange incoming switch-deals as the Bulgarians have done in fertilizers and chemicals (from West Germany), the higher price contains a brokerage component.

NOTES

1. See, for example, Ministry of Commerce, Review of Pakistan's Trade with East Europe, July 1964-June 1969 (Islamabad, 1970), p. 5.

2. It is ironic that the TCP, set up in 1966 primarily to confront the EBC foreign trade organizations with something approaching equal market power, should perform exceptionally badly. On the basis of information supplied by the organization itself and by Karachi shippers it appears that the average f.o.b price paid by Bulgarian and Polish importers for cotton grey sheeting 38 inches in width in 1968/69, was no more than 5.3 and 3.5 percent respectively above the price paid by French importers, and that Bulgaria paid 1.5 percent less than French importers for similar sheeting 50 inches wide. China bought grey cotton yarn 21/1 in hanks at a 14.2-percent discount compared with the price paid by Hong Kong; and Russia bought Basmati rice at a 2.3-percent discount off the convertible currency (Persian Gulf) price in 1967/68, a 17.7-percent discount in 1968/69, and an 11.1-percent discount in 1969/70, although this last has as much to do with the peculiarities of the captive Persian Gulf market as with Russian-TCP relations.

3. See Gordon Winston, "Over-invoicing Underutilization and Distorted Industrial Growth," Pakistan Development Review, Winter 1970, pp. 405-21, for an anatomy of the analogous although, in its day, vastly more important capital flight via imports.

If the insistence of a rumor can be considered a proxy for fact, the Bulgarians run a thoroughly "Western" system of inducements, not excluding an Embassy (in London) which hands out "commissions," "fees," "expenses," etc., in pounds sterling to agents, cousins, and partners of their Pakistan business associates. As for the rest of the EBC's, a number of Pakistani officials and some private exporters believe that the normal 5 to 10 percent gap between consignment and letter-of-credit values provides a loophole, via rigged claims settled out of court as it were, for capital flight as well as for easing the lives of some EBC officials. But a separate study would need to be made before firm conclusions could be drawn.

4. None of the five annual trade plans concluded with Russia between 1965 and 1969, and the only one of the three Rice Barter Deals signed between 1966 and 1968 had been completed by February 1970, the date of the last available series of Ministry of Commerce Implementations Reports. Russian trade is no exception.

5. See Michael Kaser, Comecon; Integration Problems of the Planned Economies, 2nd. ed. (London: Oxford University Press for the Royal Institute of International Affairs, 1967), p. 181.

6. An early mission observed: "Technomachexport agreed to supply the unit price of the cards (for card engines) but we have not received any information as yet." "Technomachexport agreed to supply the detailed reason for the price increase (of a basic spinning unit) but as of today we have not received any." "Technomachexport have agreed to supply a complete list of spares, accessories along with the price. . . . The list is still awaited." (A. K. N. Ahmed, K. A. Jafri, and M. A. Rauf, Report on the Visit of [sic] Textile Mills in U.S.S.R, November 15-30, 1966, n.p. (Karachi IDBP, n.d.[1966] (mimeo)). The Report's muted exasperation with EBC pricing policy and with the Russians' in particular, has been echoed time and again in discussions at the External Trade Division CSO, the Evaluation Division of the Customs Department, and the Foreign Exchange Section State Bank of Pakistan.

7. Interview with Major-General Faruqi, Managing Director, Oil and Gas Development Corporation, Karachi.

8. Interviews with operatives, the senior engineer, and the chief of operations, Pakistan Industrial Technical Assistance Centre (PITAC), Lahore.

9. M. F. Hussain and S. Hasan, Report on the Visit of IDBP Engineers to the East European Countries n.p. (Karachi: IDBP, n.d. [1967]) (mimeo).

10. Ahmed, Jafri, and Rauf, op. cit.

11. The latter's electrical machinery, possibly because a great deal of it is made under West European licence, is considered a "best buy" with the single reservation that it has so far been in service for only a small proportion of its expected life. (Interviews with the managing director, Power, Water and Power Development Agency (WAPDA), Lahore, and his technical and financial aides.)

12. Trade Opportunities in Eastern Europe (Karachi: Shirazi Investments Limited, n.d. [1966]), p. 12. An important businessmen's delegation that toured the European EBC's the previous autumn had been less restrained: "40 to 50 percent of our entire third Five-Year plan can be financed out of these countries at 30 to 40 percent cheaper in cost." Excerpts from the report, Finance and Industry, December 1965, p. 33. [Emphasis in the original.]

13. Aid or Trade, n.p. (Karachi: Shirazi Investments Limited,
n.d. [1969]), p. 129.

14. The quote from Shirazi's Aid or Trade was echoed in many
interviews.

15. Ministry of Commerce, Review, p. 12.

5

Early in 1970 the Russian trade representative in Pakistan drew attention to "problems of the barter trade between the two countries":

> The parties have been conscious of temporary difficulties in exploring markets for new items, adjustment of balances etc. Pakistani importers have sometimes been slow in buying Soviet goods, mainly machinery and equipment [and] Pakistani exporters have to get acquainted with Soviet consumers' demand.[1]

He might, with equal justice, have reversed "Soviet" and "Pakistan," for from the Pakistan side, "the main hurdle in the promotion of [East European] machinery imports is the lack of aggressiveness of their representatives in Pakistan."[2] And he might have gone on through a long list of complaints on quality, on procedure, on discrimination and dilatoriness, for bilateral trade takes place against a background of sustained and bitter recrimination.

It is natural. The fact that a formal long-term agreement exists invites comparison with performance. More substantially, there are real economic incompatabilities that no agreement could smoothe away. If anything, the bilateral trade pacts bring them quickly to the surface by boosting the volume of trade and wrenching it into unaccustomed geographical and commodity patterns.

SUPPLY

Ostensibly neither side will or can supply goods of the

quality and in the quantity the other wants and neither wants what the other has to sell in the quantity and of the quality in which it is offered.

Pakistan places a rigid quota on exports of the traditional con-vertible-currency-earning raw materials, jute and cotton. All of the EBC's want more, either absolutely or in proportion to their total off-take. Most have tried to shift unfilled quotas under other heads to these two commodities. But the Government of Pakistan has stood its ground: "The existing ratio between [traditional and nontraditional exports is] a basic policy" even if the growth of trade is retarded as a result.[3] Also blocked—inexplicably in view of the existence of idle capacity in the industry—is cotton yarn, wanted by Czechoslovakia, Hungary, and Poland to ease their planned shifts toward the finishing end of the textiles industry.

Nontraditional exports run into difficulties of a different kind. Although a great deal has been done to set up the "appropriate frame-works backed by adequate financial arrangements" whose absence was once held responsible for the low level of trade with the EBC's (and the Afro-Asian countries);[4] and although exports of manufactures have been encouraged lavishly through the bonus voucher system, primary products exports are still easier to service with marketing, transport, financial, and similar facilities than are manufactures.

More significantly, many of the manufactures Pakistan wishes to promote suffer from real inelasticities in supply, at least in the short run. In leather footwear the Russians have found a limit of about 150,000 pairs beyond which supplies are uncertain, compared with the 30 million pairs they are reported to have ordered from Czechoslovakia at the Moscow Footwear Fair in 1970, (Obuv '70). The Romanians complain bitterly that they have developed new export lines for Pakistan and have set internationally acceptable standards of quality—in hand-made carpets, leather products, and made-up garments for example—only to find supplies dried up when other buyers entered the market. Mica exports have a ready market but an inelatic out put, and so on.

The constraints on supply sustain a rare unanimity among EBC trade officials about the low quality of Pakistan exports, manufacturers in particular.* They all complain about it. Some of them have returned individual consignments—of shirts (Russia, Hungary) of sports

----

*The quality of raw cotton exports have also come in for a drub-bing in interviews.

goods (Hungary). Some have stopped importing certain products altogether (surgical goods to Romania for example). Others have with- held payment on imports of footwear, textiles, almost anything in fact; and many have installed quality controllers in Pakistan (tanning, foot- wear manufacturing). Even the international inspection agencies have been dragged in: The Hungarians for example, have refused to deal with the Pakistan Inspection Corporation on grounds that it is in the pay of exporters, but have had their own nominees, the Swiss-based General Superintendents, rejected because they and the exporters were, in the latter's words, "not on good terms."[5]

Pakistan trade delegations to East Europe have echoed the com- plaints, couching their optimism about trade prospects in reserve;[6] and the government has repeated them at every turn.[7] Improvements have been made and more are in the making; EBC buyers are beginning to distinguish between best and cheapest buys. But there is a limit beyond which they are unlikely to go, for the more the EBC's approxi- mate Western markets in quality requirements the less they will retain their present charm. The moment Pakistan manufacturers find they can no longer sit back and wait for orders to emerge from confabula- tions in Islamabad, they will rediscover the seductions of exporting to convertible currency markets.

Pakistan's supply inelasticities are not the only ones. The EBC's are, as was shown above, very reluctant to include raw materials in their export schedules, and although they have been nudged into supply- ing increasing amounts, SITC (Standard International Trade Classifica- tion) Sections 0-5 covered on average no more than 33 percent of all imports from the EBC's in the last half of the 1960's.[8] Machinery supplies are easier, but not without problems—mainly those of quality and specifications and have been dealt with. But sometimes they are related to policy—the right equipment often exists, only not for export, as in the case of bookbinding machinery and large baking plants from Russia.[9]

DEMAND

There are also constraints on demand. Where consumer choice exists—Russian television sets in Pakistan, for example, or Pakistan sports goods in Yugoslavia—the commodities move slowly. This is to be expected, since barter deals are concluded to counter just such a situation. But even within the captive markets formed by agreement, a lot can go wrong.

The East Europeans are finding it difficult to include complete plants in barter deals; Pakistan wants them under credit. They have found it impossible to enter the tractor market, which is protected by a seemingly impregnable "standardization" requirement. Nothing they have attempted could bring definition and product into harmony. Romania can find no room for its oil-drilling equipment in a market shared by the Russians and the Americans (and British) each with "their own organization" (the Russian-financed Oil and Gas Development Corporation and the largely U.S. British-controlled private sector). The same goes for petrochemicals. And all of the EBC's with partial exception made for Poland and Yugoslavia which manufacture a wide range of West German equipment under licence, have met one frustration after another in selling standard machinery items.

Conversely, Pakistan has encountered difficulties in marketing some of its new manufactures and nontraditional items even when they were available, as in the case of textile products, fruit juices, footwear, surgical goods, spectacle frames, machine tools, electric fans, and electric motors.

Sometimes bad quality has been advanced in explanation. Sometimes price, or the inadequancy of the product range, or the lack of assurance about continued supplies, or servicing arrangements. Sometimes there has been more than one reason; but underlying them all there has usually been a current of pressure on Pakistan to make the rupee-generating purchases that would trigger off matching purchases from the EBC's.

The result has been a growing drag on the increase in trade, not only in the minds of trade officials but in fact—the strong upward thrust of 1962/63-1966/67 shown in Table II-2 was, it seems, petering out by the end of the decade. And while it is true that ten years are a paltry statistical base for economic conclusion, particularly years that span the Indo-Pakistan War, the closure of the Suez Canal, the social and political spasm that ended the Ayub regime, and the period of commercial lethargy that ensured, there are good grounds, in addition to those already given, for believing that demand on both sides will continue to flag.*

One ground is the growing burden for Pakistan of debt servicing on both open commercial account and hidden military account. The former

---

*See the previous section and Chapter 3.

pre-empts some 22 percent of exports to the EBC's as it is (Tables II-1 and 32). Together they must constitute a fair proportion of the resources Pakistan feels able to free for this trade. Assuming no change in the EBC share of total exports and no change in the volume of credit, servicing of the commercial debt alone might have been expected to absorb 26 percent of export earnings from the EBC's during the fourth, lame-duck Five Year Plan, 1970-75.[10] Of course the EBC's could offset the payment squeeze by providing further credit on terms acceptable to Pakistan, but that would require an immense, and new, general commitment on their part.

In the early 1960's when the decisions to barter were incubating, the parties' immediate interests were clear enough. The Russians' seemed to lie in preventing Pakistan and China on the one hand and the United States and India on the other from achieving too close a political alignment. For China, closer links with Pakistan meant discomforting both the U.S. and Russia, while simultaneously threatening India and opening for herself a valuable window on the world. As for East Europe (and Russia to a less extent), Pakistan looked like an attractive candidate for making good some of the enormous losses incurred in the collapse of their trade with China, as well as a natural target for their general policy of trade (and political) diversification.[11] For its part, Pakistan was eager to reduce a dependence on the United States which was becoming embarrassing now that Indo-U.S. relations had improved and pressure was being exerted to reduce the Pakistan military establishment. On a more mundane level, Pakistan saw in closer relations with the EBC's an opportunity to counter the gradual erosion of its trade surplus with them,[12] as well as some insurance against the strong protectionist tide that seemed to be encroaching on Western Europe.[13]

Many of these motives have weakened since and while some EBC spokesmen occasionally refer to the desirability of closer integration between Pakistan and their own economies, as the Czechoslovaks have done[14] or the Russians,[15] they do so more in the spirit of extending bilateral trading principles to what seems to be their logical conclusion than in pursuit of practical goals.[16] In practice the EBC's show a common indifference to Pakistan's economic aims and to its "dynamic comparative advantage." The Russians, for example, have been unwilling to accommodate Pakistan sports goods for fear of losing their autarky;[17] they and the Hungarians have demanded polyester, not cotton, shirts as part of their barter exchange;[18] and with the Czechoslovaks they have announced their firm intention of buying raw materials from Pakistan, leaving their plans for importing manufactures vague.[19]

The pressures set up by quick economic maturation in the European EBC's for closer economic contact among themselves and between them and the West are clearly very strong, stronger than the pulls toward complementarity with Pakistan or similar economies. But even if this were not so, suggestions for closer integration would hold little attraction for Pakistan in current circumstances. Not only is the economic success of the EBC's less apparent than it once was, or the size disparity between the Pakistan industrial economy and that of the smallest, least industrialized EBC uncomfortably great and growing, or even that the implied shift to tight planning and state enterprise would strain the existing fragile social and political structure in Pakistan to the breaking point, but the experience of bilateral trade with the EBC's has revealed hidden costs that no government could ignore, unless it were brought to do so by a new, and heavy, injection of credit, this time presumably on military account.

Some of these costs have been mentioned. Others, for example the loss occasioned by exporting manufactures with a high convertible currency import content,[20] or the loss occasioned by assimilating elements of the highly unstable EBC production cycle,[21] must wait for further research before they can be fully established. But failing a new and costly initiative from the EBC's they weigh heavily against further buoyancy in Pakistan-EBC trade.

NOTES

1. A.E. Erokhin, "Pakistan-U.S.S.R. Trade Relations, Consolidated Barter Agreement Mutually Advantageous," Pakistan Economist, IX, no. 3 (March 1970) 62.

2. M.F. Hussain and S. Hasan, Report on the Visit of IDBP Engineers to the East European Countries, n.p. (Karachi: IDBP, n.d. [1967]) (mimeo).

3. Summary of a discussion between the Yugoslav and Pakistan Trade Delagations, Islamabad, July 15-20, 1968, prepared by D. Martinovic, leader of the Yugoslav Delegation. This refusal is particularly interesting since the original Protocol. signed in September 1966, had already been extended twice and was to be extended yet again because of "the unsatisfactory progress of utilization of the quota against various sub-groups under Group "B" [nontraditional items] of Schedule "A" [Pakistan exports]." The Yugoslavs had proposed

transferring the original ceilings for Basmati rice and ores and minerals to raw cotton.

4. Sartaj Aziz, then chief, International Economics Section, Planning Commission, "Future Trends in Pakistan's International Trade," Trade Journal, June-July 1964, pp. 35-37. The Trading Corporation of Pakistan was set up in 1966, and the Export Promotion Bureau in 1963.

5. This paragraph is based on interviews.

6. "There are prospects for our medium and better quality sports goods . . . provided standard is maintained . . . definite prospects of good business [in surgical instruments] but only through high standard and quaranteed quality." Monsoor Elahie, Pakistan's Barter Trade, Research Report No. 2, (Karachi: Pakistan Institute of Development Economics, April, 1963) p. 7 (Mimeo)"; . . . a big and good market . . . if our manufacturers take special care in producing quality goods." (Mr. Salam, quoted in Trade and Industry, January 1967, p. 398); and so on and on.

7. For example: "Leather shoes hold out promise, provided the production adjusts itself to meet the specific requirements of these countries for the waterproof shoes. . . . Export of minor items like sports goods and surgical instruments is beset with the problem of standardization and quality." Ministry of Commerce, Review of Pakistan's Trade with East Europe, July 1964-June 1969 (Islamabad, 1970), p. 7.

8. The Ministry of Commerce's claim to having pushed up the proportion of raw materials imported from East Europe and Russia from under 20 percent to 50 percent in the three years 1965/66-1967/68 has less to do with reality than with a compliant nomenclature that includes pharmaceutical or petroleum products, for example, under raw materials; and their optimism for the future has a lot to do with such indications of good will as Czechoslovakia's agreement to list coal, coke, iron, and steel without having made arrangements for their release and without having, in the words of one of their trade officials, "the slightest idea as to where they are to come from."

9. Hussain and Hassan, op. cit., pp. 5, 6.

10. Tables II-1 and 32; and Pakistan Planning Commission The Fourth Five Year Plan 1970-75 (Islamabad, July 1970), p. 62, Table 4.

11. Trade between East Europe and "the socialist countries of

Asia" (mainly China) fell from 10.5 percent of East Europe's imports
in 1960 to 1.9 percent in 1969, more than two thirds of the fall occuring
by 1963. See UNCTAD, Recent Trends Review of International Trade
and Development 1969/70, Part One: Recent Trends in Trade and
Development, TD/B/309 (Geneva: UNCTAD, August 7, 1970), p. 16;
Michael Kaser, Comecon: Integration Problems of the Planned
Economies, Znd. ed. (London: Oxford University Press for the Royal
Institute of International Affairs, 1967), p. 144.

12. See Mansoor Elahic, op.cit. Table 1, p. 4; Ministry of Commerce, Review op. cit; p. 1.

13. See Shirazi, Aid or Trade (Karachi: Shirazi, Investments
limited, n.d. [1967]), pp. 17 and 26 for a statement of the facts as seen
by the private sector; and for the general background, Michael Kidron,
"From High Indignation to Indifference, Asian Commonwealth Attitudes
to Britain's Entry in Pierre Uri, ed., From Commonwealth to Common
Market (Harmondsworth: Penguin, 1970).

14. See Ellahie, op. cit., p. 21.

15. M. Hassan, "The Dynamic Role of Barter Trade in Our
Economic Development," Dawn, August 7, 1970.

16. Proposals for dovetailing activity between EBC's and underdeveloped countries range from general, theoretical statements to
single ad hoc suggestions, neither of which carry much conviction.
At one end of the spectrum is Zevin's distinction between "two periods
in the formation of this new type of ['equal product exchange'] economic
relationship between Socialist and developing countries": one characterized by the "intensification of economic relations, increase in the volun
of trade due mainly to larger exchange of traditional goods," and a
second to be characterized mainly by "wide co-operation in production
and by the involvement of new goods in the exchange process." (Zevin,
op. cit.)

At the other end of the spectrum lie Popescu's suggestions for
direct Romanian investment in underdeveloped countries and for joint
production with them (Petre N. Popescu, Trade Prospects in Socialist
Countries, Romania: Conditions, Policies, Approaches, a study presented to UNCTAD, Trade and Development Board. Tenth Session,
Geneva, August 26, 1970. TD/B/304 [Geneva: UNCTAD, June 16,
1970], pp. 33 and 34 [mimeo]); and Pravda et al's listing of intergovern-
mental bodies "to follow up the implementation of the agreements in
force" (Miroslav Pravda, Vladimir Novacek, and Zdenek Venera,

Trade Prospects in Socialist Countries. Czechoslovakia: Conditions, Policies, Approaches, a study presented to UNCTAD, ibid., p. 31).

17. S.H. Akhtar, Report of the Pakistan Trade Delegation to U.S.S.R. Hungary and Poland From 8th April to 29th April 1967, n.p., n.d. (duplicated), p. 14.

18. Ibid., pp. 12 and 23.

19. For example, from the president of the Czechoslovak Chamber of Commerce and Industry on their first tour of the country, early in 1963: "Czechoslovakia could buy from Pakistan some volume of semi-processed and finished goods but must concentrate mainly on the purchase of raw materials." Quoted in Trade Opportunities in East Europe (Karachi: Shirazi Investments Limited, n.d. [1966]), p. 27. Similarly from a Russia trade source: "The U.S.S.R. is going to increase its purchases of . . . cotton and jute in Pakistan" as well as increasing "purchases of manufactures and semi-manufactures in developing countries" Lev L. Klochkovsky, Trade Prospects in Socialist Countries. Union of Soviet Republics: Conditions, Policies, Prospects, a study presented to UNCTAD, Trade and Development Board, Tenth Session, Geneva, August 26, 1970, TD/B/303 (Geneva: UNCTAD, June 26, 1970), p. 33. [Emphasis added.]

20. Unpublished reports prepared by the Cost Accounts Organization, Ministry of Finance, on individual exporting firms show a high proportion of imported inputs in total export value in products of major interest to the EBC's: spectacle frames, 63-79 percent; surgical instruments, 37-78 percent; footwear, 15-39 percent. An unpublished partial analysis prepared on similar lines by the Export Promotion Bureau shows relatively low value added in manufactures of special interest to the EBC's: spectacle frames, 21-37 percent; cutlery, 28 percent; "engineering items," 28 percent. Without further elaboration, however, these results should be considered suggestive rather than conclusive.

21. A preliminary statistical analysis of raw jute, raw cotton, and rice exports suggests that the EBC's are substantially less stable than Western countries as markets for primary commodities. This accords with the general experience (see, much to do with their relative smallness as markets, their policy of keeping stocks low, and their monopoly of foreign trade. In exports of manufactures where the first consideration does not apply, the prime source of instability seems to be the plan-fulfilment cycle typical of the EBC's. In Pakistan footwear manufacturers with a substantial interest in the Russian market are acutely conscious of that cycle.

GENERAL
NOTES FOR TABLES

The original source for statistics, either direct or derived, is the Central Statistical Office of Pakistan, unless otherwise specified.

All years are fiscal years - i. e. , July 1 to June 30.

Pak.   = Pakistan; E. P. = East Pakistan; W. P. = West Pakistan

PSTC   = Pakistan Standard Trade Classification

—   = less than 0. 01 percent

n. e. s. = not elsewhere specified

NOTE FOR TABLES II-17 - II-26

The Pakistan Standard Trade Classification has been revised and amended a number of times in the course of the decade covered by our series, notably in 1963 when a seven-digit classification was dropped in favor of a six-digit one, and in 1966 when a major re-classification took place.

Year-by-year comparability of individual items has suffered thereby and should be undertaken with caution. The yearly price premium comparisons and the general conclusions to be drawn from the tables are not affected.

TABLE II-1

Share of EBC's in Pakistan's Trade, 1960/61-1969/70
(million rupees)

	1960/61			1961/62			1962/63			1963/64		
	Pak.	E.P.	W.P.	Pak.	E.P.	W.P.	Pak.	E.P.	W.P.	Pak.	E.P.	W.P.
1. Total Trade	4,986.8	2,273.5	2,713.3	4,951.7	2,172.8	2,779.0	6,066.6	2,267.8	3,798.8	6,729.1	2,672.7	4,056.4
2. Trade with EBC's	224.9	121.1	103.8	180.5	108.1	72.4	200.3	104.5	95.9	398.9	175.2	223.7
3. Trade with European EBC's	99.5	71.2	28.3	118.7	78.6	40.0	89.4	54.3	35.0	128.1	84.6	43.4
4. Trade with U.S.S.R.	35.1	14.1	21.0	31.3	18.6	12.7	44.8	22.2	22.6	53.4	25.5	27.9
5. Trade with China	90.3	35.8	54.5	30.5	10.9	19.6	66.2	28.0	38.2	217.5	65.1	152.4
6. Trade with EBC's as % of Total Trade	4.5	5.3	3.8	3.7	5.0	2.6	3.3	4.6	2.5	5.9	6.5	5.5
7. Trade with European EBC's as % of Trade with EBC's	44.2	58.8	27.3	65.8	72.7	55.3	44.6	52.0	36.6	32.1	48.3	19.4
8. Trade with U.S.S.R. as % of Trade with EBC's	15.6	11.7	20.2	17.3	17.2	17.6	22.4	21.2	23.6	13.4	14.6	12.5
9. Trade with China as % of Trade with EBC's	40.1	29.5	52.5	16.9	10.1	27.1	33.0	26.8	39.9	54.5	37.2	68.1
10. Total Trade Index at Current Price (1965/66 = 100)	72.0	80.0	66.4	71.5	76.5	68.1	87.6	79.8	93.0	97.2	94.0	99.3
11. EBC's Trade Index at Current Prices (1956/66 = 100)	35.5	43.5	29.3	28.5	38.8	20.4	31.7	37.6	27.0	63.0	63.0	63.1
12. European EBC's Trade Index at Current Prices (1965/66 = 100)	39.7	62.6	20.7	47.4	69.1	29.3	35.7	47.7	25.7	51.2	74.4	31.8
13. U.S.S.R. Trade Index at Current Prices (1965/66 = 100)	23.8	45.9	18.0	21.2	60.4	10.9	30.3	72.0	19.3	36.1	82.8	23.8
14. China's Trade Index at Current Prices (1965/66 = 100)	38.5	26.8	54.0	13.0	8.2	19.4	28.2	21.0	37.9	92.7	48.7	151.0
15. Total Trade Index at Constant Prices (1965/66 = 100)	78.1	79.0	76.3	81.4	88.2	76.5	99.3	96.1	102.3	109.5	114.8	107.7
16. EBC's Trade Index at Constant Prices (1965/66 = 100)	38.6	43.0	33.6	32.5	45.0	23.0	35.9	45.2	29.8	71.1	76.9	68.4
17. European EBC's Trade Index at Constant Prices (1965/66 = 100)	43.1	61.8	23.8	53.9	80.0	33.0	40.5	57.5	28.2	57.6	90.8	34.5
18. U.S.S.R. Trade Index at Constant Prices (1965/66 = 100)	25.8	45.3	20.6	24.1	69.9	12.2	34.4	86.8	21.3	40.7	101.2	25.8
19. China's Trade Index at Constant Prices (1965/66 = 100)	41.7	26.4	62.0	14.8	9.5	21.9	32.0	25.2	41.7	104.5	59.5	163.7

20. Total Exports	1,799.4	1,259.2	540.2	1,843.4	1,300.6	542.9	2,247.3	1,249.2	998.1	2,299.1	1,224.1	1,075.0
21. Exports to Eastern Bloc Countries	157.9	110.7	47.2	102.7	93.2	9.5	109.9	81.7	28.2	275.6	119.3	156.2
22. Exports to European EBC's (Excluding U.S.S.R.)	68.9	68.3	0.6	73.2	71.8	1.4	44.4	44.1	0.3	96.3	72.7	23.6
23. Exports to U.S.S.R.	14.2	14.1	0.1	18.8	18.5	0.3	22.5	22.1	0.4	12.9	12.3	0.6
24. Exports to China	74.8	28.3	46.5	10.6	2.9	7.7	42.9	15.4	27.5	166.4	34.4	132.0
25. Exports to EBC's as % of Total Exports	8.8	8.8	8.7	5.6	7.2	1.7	4.9	6.5	2.8	12.0	9.8	14.5
26. Exports to European EBC's (Excluding U.S.S.R.) as % of Exports to EBC's	43.6	61.7	1.2	71.3	77.0	15.2	40.4	54.0	1.0	35.0	60.9	15.1
27. Exports to U.S.S.R. as % of Exports to EBC's	9.0	12.7	0.3	18.3	19.9	3.3	20.5	27.1	1.4	4.7	10.3	0.4
28. Exports to China as % of Exports to EBC's	47.4	25.6	98.5	10.4	3.2	81.5	39.1	18.9	97.6	60.4	28.8	84.5
29. Total Imports	3,187.4	1,014.3	2,173.1	3,108.3	872.2	2,236.1	3,819.3	1,018.6	2,800.7	4,429.9	1,448.5	2,981.4
30. Imports from EBC's	67.0	10.4	56.6	77.8	14.9	62.9	90.5	22.8	67.7	123.3	55.9	67.4
31. Imports from European EBC's (Excluding U.S.S.R.)	30.6	2.9	27.7	45.5	6.9	38.6	44.9	10.2	34.8	31.7	11.9	19.8
32. Imports from U.S.S.R.	20.9	—	20.9	12.5	—	12.4	22.2	—	22.2	40.5	13.2	27.3
33. Imports from China	15.5	7.5	8.0	19.9	8.0	11.9	23.3	12.6	10.7	51.1	30.7	20.4
34. Imports from EBC's as % of Total Imports	2.1	1.0	2.6	2.5	1.7	2.8	2.4	2.2	2.4	2.8	3.9	2.3
35. Imports from European EBC's (Excluding U.S.S.R.) as % of Imports from EBC's	45.7	27.5	49.0	58.4	46.0	61.4	49.7	44.7	51.4	25.7	21.4	29.3
36. Imports from U.S.S.R. as % of Imports from EBC's	31.2	0.6	36.9	16.0	0.4	19.7	24.6	0.1	32.5	32.8	23.7	40.4
37. Imports from China as % of Imports from EBC's	23.1	71.9	14.1	25.6	53.6	18.9	25.7	55.2	15.8	41.4	55.0	30.2

(Continued)

TABLE II-1 (Continued)

	1964/65			1965/66			1966/67			1967/68			1968/69			1969/70		
	Pak.	E.P.	W.P.	Pak.	E.P.	W.P.	Pak.	E.P.	W.P.	Pak.	E.P.	W.P.	Pak.	E.P.	W.P.	Pak.	E.P.	W.P.
1. Total Trade	7,782.0	2,970.0	4,812.0	6,926.1	2,842.2	4,083.9	8,105.0	3,141.2	4,963.7	7,779.3	2,807.3	4,972.1	8,109.8	3,383.3	4,746.5	8,369.6	3,475.9	4,893.6
2. Trade with EBC's	555.4	253.2	302.3	632.7	278.1	354.5	1,001.5	425.2	576.3	767.2	281.7	485.2	1,190.1	525.7	664.4	972.4	456.9	515.5
3. Trade with European EBC's	207.1	93.8	113.3	250.4	113.8	136.6	347.5	139.0	208.5	313.7	109.8	203.6	689.6	292.6	396.9	528.5	229.7	298.8
4. Trade with U.S.S.R.	69.1	10.4	58.7	147.8	30.8	117.0	286.3	76.0	210.3	229.4	35.0	194.4	244.1	70.0	174.1	195.0	81.4	113.6
5. Trade with China	279.2	148.9	130.3	234.5	133.6	100.9	367.6	210.2	157.4	224.2	137.0	87.2	256.5	163.2	93.4	248.9	145.8	103.1
6. Trade with EBC's as % of Total Trade	7.1	8.5	6.3	9.1	9.8	8.7	12.4	13.5	11.6	9.9	10.0	9.8	14.7	15.6	14.0	11.6	13.2	10.5
7. Trade with European EBC's as % of Trade with EBC's	37.3	37.1	37.5	39.6	40.9	38.5	34.7	32.7	36.2	40.9	39.0	42.0	57.9	55.7	59.7	54.4	50.3	58.0
8. Trade with U.S.S.R. as % of Trade with EBC's	12.5	4.1	19.4	23.4	11.1	33.0	28.6	17.9	36.5	29.9	12.4	40.1	20.5	13.3	26.2	20.1	17.8	22.0
9. Trade with China as % of Trade with EBC's	50.3	58.8	43.1	37.1	49.0	28.5	36.7	49.4	27.3	29.2	48.6	18.0	21.6	31.0	14.1	25.6	31.9	20.0
10. Total Trade Index at Current Price (1965/66 = 100)	112.4	104.5	107.8	100.0	100.0	100.0	117.0	110.5	121.5	112.3	98.8	121.8	117.1	118.3	116.2	120.8	122.3	119.8
11. EBC's Trade Index at Current Prices (1965/66 = 100)	87.8	91.0	85.3	100.0	100.0	100.0	158.3	152.9	162.5	121.3	101.3	136.9	188.1	189.0	187.4	153.7	164.3	145.4
12. European EBC's Trade Index at Current Prices (1965/66 = 100)	82.7	82.5	82.9	100.0	100.0	100.0	138.8	122.1	152.7	125.3	96.5	149.1	275.4	257.2	290.6	211.1	201.9	218.7
13. U.S.S.R. Trade Index at Current Prices (1965/66 = 100)	46.8	33.9	50.2	100.0	100.0	100.0	193.8	247.1	179.8	155.2	113.6	166.2	165.2	227.4	148.8	132.0	264.4	97.1
14. China's Trade Index at Current Prices (1965/66 = 100)	119.1	111.5	129.1	100.0	100.0	100.0	156.8	157.4	156.0	95.6	102.5	86.4	109.4	122.1	92.5	106.2	109.2	162.2
15. Total Trade Index at Constant Prices (1965/66 = 100)	117.4	113.6	120.6	100.0	100.0	100.0	115.6	111.4	119.0	117.6	106.1	126.6	112.9	116.1	113.2	113.4	120.7	111.3
16. EBC's Trade Index at Constant Prices (1965/66 = 100)	91.8	99.0	87.2	100.0	100.0	100.0	156.3	154.1	159.1	127.0	108.8	142.3	182.7	185.5	182.6	144.3	162.1	135.0
17. European EBC's Trade Index at Constant Prices (1965/66 = 100)	86.4	89.6	84.9	100.0	100.0	100.0	137.1	123.1	149.4	131.2	103.7	155.0	267.5	252.3	283.1	198.1	199.2	203.1
18. U.S.S.R. Trade Index at Constant Prices (1965/66 = 100)	48.9	36.9	51.3	100.0	100.0	100.0	191.4	249.1	176.0	162.6	122.0	172.8	160.4	223.1	145.0	128.9	260.9	90.2
19. China's Trade Index at Constant Prices (1965/66 = 100)	124.4	121.2	132.1	100.0	100.0	100.0	154.8	158.7	152.7	100.1	110.1	89.8	106.3	119.9	90.1	99.6	107.7	94.8

20.	Total Exports	2,407.7	1,268.1	1,139.6	2,717.7	1,514.1	1,203.6	2,912.7	1,574.7	1,338.1	3,124.6	1,479.8	1,644.8	3,239.8	1,539.9	1,699.9	3,271.4	1,662.8	1,608.6
21.	Exports to Eastern Bloc Countries	286.7	187.8	98.9	357.2	187.3	169.9	501.0	244.8	256.2	326.7	121.6	204.8	538.6	242.8	295.9	546.2	224.6	321.6
22.	Exports to European EBC's (Excluding U.S.S.R.)	95.6	80.41	15.2	122.5	85.0	37.5	162.7	100.0	62.7	137.5	41.4	95.8	321.6	146.6	175.0	324.5	92.9	231.6
23.	Exports to U.S.S.R.	11.7	9.1	2.6	80.0	20.2	59.8	130.4	20.8	109.6	79.4	16.8	62.6	109.1	30.1	79.0	83.8	28.6	55.3
24.	Exports to China	179.4	98.3	81.1	154.7	82.1	72.6	207.9	124.0	83.9	109.9	63.4	46.4	107.9	66.1	41.8	137.8	103.2	34.6
25.	Exports to EBC's as % of Total Exports	11.9	14.8	8.8	13.1	12.4	14.1	17.2	15.5	19.2	10.5	8.2	12.5	16.6	15.8	17.4	16.7	13.5	20.0
26.	Exports to European EBC's (Excluding U.S.S.R.) as % of Exports to EBC's	33.4	42.8	15.4	34.3	45.4	22.1	32.5	40.9	24.5	42.1	24.1	46.8	59.7	60.4	59.2	59.4	41.1	72.0
27.	Exports to U.S.S.R. as % of Exports to EBC's	4.1	4.8	2.6	22.4	10.8	35.2	26.0	8.5	42.8	24.3	13.8	30.6	20.3	12.4	26.7	15.4	12.7	17.2
28.	Exports to China as % of Exports to EBC's	62.6	52.32	82.0	43.3	43.8	42.7	41.5	50.7	32.7	33.6	52.2	23.8	20.0	27.2	14.1	25.2	45.9	10.8
29.	Total Imports	5,374.2	1,701.8	3,672.4	4,208.3	1,328.1	2,880.3	5,192.3	1,566.6	3,625.7	4,654.7	1,327.5	3,327.2	4,870.0	1,823.4	3,046.6	5,098.1	1,813.1	3,285.1
30.	Imports from EBC's	268.7	65.4	203.4	275.5	90.8	184.6	500.5	180.4	320.1	440.5	160.11	280.4	651.5	283.0	368.5	426.3	232.3	193.9
31.	Imports from European EBC's (Excluding U.S.S.R.)	111.4	13.4	98.1	127.9	28.8	99.1	184.8	39.0	145.8	176.2	68.4	107.8	368.0	146.1	221.9	204.0	136.8	67.1
32.	Imports from U.S.S.R.	57.5	1.4	56.1	67.7	10.5	57.2	156.0	55.3	100.7	150.0	18.2	131.8	135.0	39.9	95.1	111.2	52.8	58.4
33.	Imports from China	99.8	50.6	49.1	79.8	51.5	28.3	159.8	86.2	73.5	114.3	73.5	40.8	148.6	97.0	51.5	111.1	42.7	68.5
34.	Imports from EBC's as % of Total Imports	5.0	3.8	5.5	6.6	6.8	6.4	9.6	11.5	8.5	9.5	12.1	8.4	13.4	15.5	12.1	8.4	12.8	5.9
35.	Imports from European EBC's (Excluding U.S.S.R.) as % of Imports from EBC's	41.5	20.5	48.2	46.1	31.7	53.7	36.9	21.6	45.6	40.0	42.7	39.6	56.5	51.6	60.2	47.9	58.9	34.6
36.	Imports from U.S.S.R. as % of Imports from EBC's	21.4	2.1	27.6	24.4	11.6	31.0	31.2	30.6	31.5	34.1	11.4	48.5	20.7	14.1	25.8	26.1	22.8	30.1
37.	Imports from China as % of Imports from EBC's	37.1	77.5	24.2	28.8	56.7	15.4	31.9	47.8	23.0	25.9	45.9	14.5	22.8	34.3	14.0	26.1	18.4	35.3

TABLE II-2

Year-to-Year Percentage Change in Pakistan's Trade Turnover with the EBC's, 1960/61-1969/70

	1960/61-61/62			1961/62-62/63			1962/63-63/64			1963/64-64/65			1964/65-65/66		
	Pak.	E.P.	W.P.	Pak.	E.P.	W.P.	Pak.	E.P.	W.P.	Pak.	E.P.	W.P.	Pak.	E.P.	W.P.
A. Current Prices															
World	-0.71	-4.43	2.42	22.52	4.37	36.70	10.92	17.85	6.78	15.65	11.12	18.63	-11.00	-4.3	-15.13
EBC's	-19.72	-10.85	-30.29	10.97	-3.22	32.48	99.12	67.78	133.28	39.23	44.48	35.15	13.91	9.87	17.30
East Europe	19.30	10.50	41.44	-24.71	-30.93	-12.49	43.30	55.83	23.90	61.73	10.84	160.91	20.89	21.29	20.57
U.S.S.R.	-10.90	31.51	-39.42	43.07	19.28	77.84	19.26	15.03	23.16	29.56	-59.03	110.63	113.77	194.61	99.38
China	-66.17	-69.45	-64.02	116.79	156.15	94.88	228.53	132.68	298.68	28.39	128.76	-14.50	-16.01	-10.31	-22.53
B. Constant Prices															
World	4.20	11.63	0.31	22.05	9.02	33.72	10.27	19.44	5.24	7.23	-1.05	11.99	-14.84	-11.98	-17.07
EBC's	-15.77	4.70	-31.71	10.56	0.53	29.57	97.95	70.05	129.88	29.12	28.65	27.56	8.99	1.04	14.63
East Europe	25.18	29.52	23.79	-24.99	-28.10	-14.38	42.46	57.94	22.11	50.07	-1.31	146.29	15.69	11.56	17.83
U.S.S.R.	-6.48	54.16	-40.68	42.47	24.14	73.98	18.46	16.60	21.40	20.15	-63.52	98.84	104.54	171.00	94.86
China	-64.49	-64.21	-64.76	115.92	166.70	90.62	226.63	135.87	292.94	19.05	103.68	-19.28	-19.63	-17.50	-24.30

| | 1965/66-66/67 | | | 1966/67-67/68 | | | 1967/68-68/69 | | | 1968/69-69/70 | | | Average Annual Change 1960/61-69/70 | | |
	Pak.	E.P.	W.P.	Pak.	E.P.	W.P.	Pak.	E.P.	W.P.	Pak.	E.P.	W.P.	Pak.	E.P.	W.P.
							A. Current Prices								
World	17.02	10.52	21.54	-4.02	-10.63	0.17	4.25	19.80	-4.53	3.20	3.36	3.10	5.92	4.83	6.77
EBC's	58.29	52.86	62.54	-23.39	-33.74	-15.80	55.13	86.61	36.93	-18.29	-13.09	-22.41	17.67	15.90	19.49
East Europe	38.78	52.65	52.65	-9.73	-20.97	-2.36	119.83	166.43	94.96	-23.36	-21.50	-24.73	20.39	13.89	29.93
U.S.S.R.	93.77	147.06	79.75	-19.89	-54.02	-7.55	6.40	100.16	-10.46	-20.10	16.30	-34.72	20.99	21.48	20.64
China	56.77	57.35	55.99	-39.03	-34.84	-44.61	14.44	19.13	7.07	-2.96	-10.62	10.42	11.93	16.90	7.34
							B. Constant Prices								
World	15.57	11.44	18.96	1.77	-4.79	6.41	-4.04	9.45	-10.54	0.48	3.91	-1.75	4.24	4.82	4.24
EBC's	56.32	54.13	59.09	-18.76	-29.40	-10.55	43.88	70.48	28.31	-21.05	-12.62	-26.06	15.79	15.89	16.70
East Europe	37.06	23.14	49.41	-4.28	-30.60	3.72	103.89	143.36	82.69	-25.95	-21.06	-28.27	18.47	13.90	26.90
U.S.S.R.	91.36	149.10	75.94	-15.05	-51.01	-1.80	-1.31	82.85	-16.08	-19.68	16.93	-37.79	19.58	21.47	17.83
China	54.82	58.65	52.68	-35.34	-30.58	-41.16	6.14	8.83	0.33	-6.24	-10.13	5.23	10.15	16.90	4.84

Source: Table II-1.

TABLE II-3

EBC's Share of Pakistan's Major Exports, 1967/68-1969/70
(thousand rupees)

PSTC Code No.	Description	Exports to the World[a]	% of Total Exports to the World	Exports to the EBC's[b]	% of Total Exports to the EBC's	Exports to EBC's as % of Exports to World	Percentage of Exports to EBC's Taken by:					
							China Amount	%	Russia Amount	%	East Europe Amount	%
0422	Rice, glazed or polished	132,816.3	4.14	24,387.1	5.37	18.36	–	–	20,386.7	83.60	4,001.5	16.41
2631	Raw cotton, other than linters	332,973.4	10.37	100,915.4	22.21	30.31	43,210.4	42.82	8,065.9	7.99	49,639.1	49.19
2640	Raw jute	750,664.8	23.37	156,354.9	34.42	20.83	68,519.8	42.82	22,848.3	14.61	64,986.9	42.57
6119	Leather; skins	102,068.4	3.18	14,266.8	3.14	13.98	–	–	2,381.6	16.69	11,885.3	83.31
6513	Cotton yarn, unbleached	160,190.1	5.00	10,684.5	2.35	6.67	4,002.7	37.46	16.4	0.15	6,648.2	62.22
6514	Cotton yarn, bleached	73,063.3	2.27	18,707.5	4.12	25.60	413.9	2.21	1,478.6	7.90	16,815.0	89.88
6521	Cotton cloth, unbleached	134,966.1	4.20	34,252.0	7.54	25.38	28.6	0.08	53.5	0.16	34,169.9	99.76
6522	Cotton cloth, bleached	84,585.1	2.63	33,611.7	7.40	39.74	67.7	0.20	13,408.0	39.89	20,135.9	59.91
6534	Jute fabrics	404,605.9	12.60	4,653.6	1.02	1.15	135.7	2.92	10.3	0.22	4,522.7	97.19
6561	Bags & sacks of textile	274,775.4	8.55	9,078.6	2.00	3.30	562.5	6.20	299.9	3.30	7,866.0	86.64
6575	Knotted carpets, rugs	41,331.7	1.29	2,117.2	0.47	5.12	–	–	18.5	0.87	2,085.4	98.50

Notes: [a] 1 percent and above of all exports to the world in each of the three years.
[b] Exports to Mongoloa are included in the EBC total.

TABLE II-4

EBC's Share of Pakistan's Major Imports, 1967/68-1969/70
(thousand rupees)

PSTC Code No.	Description	Imports from the World*	% of Total Imports from the World	Imports from the EBC's	% of Imports from the EBC's	Imports from the EBC's as % of Imports from World	Imports from EBC's Supplied by: China Amount	China %	Russia Amount	Russia %	East Europe Amount	East Europe %
5310	Organic dyestuffs	53,937.7	1.11	13,411.9	2.46	24.87	5,275.4	39.33	399.6	2.98	7,736.8	57.69
5417	Medicaments	60,725.3	1.25	5,081.4	0.93	8.37	1,435.5	28.25	325.6	6.41	3,320.0	65.34
5611	Nitrogenous fertilizer	175,301.7	3.60	36,567.6	6.70	20.86	3.9	0.01	14,144.5	38.68	22,419.2	61.31
5992	Insecticides	75,399.7	1.55	4,761.0	0.87	6.31	426.9	8.97	23.4	0.49	4,310.9	90.55
6725	Blooms, billets	89,671.0	1.84	10,297.6	1.89	11.48	117.2	1.14	10,128.2	98.35	52.3	0.51
6741	Universal heavy plates	143,716.2	2.95	2,654.2	0.49	1.85	468.0	17.62	22.0	0.83	2,164.5	81.55
6911	Finished structures of steel	71,997.3	1.48	12,625.4	2.31	17.54	68.0	0.54	2,544.7	20.16	10,012.7	79.40
7125	Tractors	82,833.1	1.70	14,608.6	2.68	17.64	–	–	13,133.0	89.90	1,475.6	10.10
7171	Textile machines	249,667.5	5.12	8,372.1	1.53	3.35	2,335.1	27.89	1,854.8	22.16	4,182.2	49.95
7184	Mining machinery	125,328.6	2.57	25,487.4	4.67	20.34	32.7	0.13	16,457.2	64.57	8,997.6	35.30
7193	Mechanical handling equipment	61,473.2	1.26	8,167.9	1.50	13.29	128.7	1.58	1,759.7	21.54	6,279.5	76.88
7198	Machinery	64,326.8	1.32	5,752.7	1.05	8.94	247.4	4.30	1,797.0	31.24	3,708.3	64.45
7199	Machinery parts	78,902.1	1.62	8,789.2	1.61	11.14	375.4	4.27	3,859.8	43.92	4,554.0	51.81
7221	Electric power machinery	94,446.7	1.94	23,261.5	4.26	24.63	544.7	2.21	1,274.8	5.46	21,442.0	91.33
7222	Switchgear	65,539.3	1.34	10,143.3	1.86	15.48	529.2	5.22	59.6	0.59	9,554.5	94.20

Note: * 1 percent and above of all imports from the world in each of the three years.

TABLE II-5

Pakistan's Exports to the EBC's by EBC Market Share,
1967/68-1969/70

76-100%			51-75%			26-50%		
PSTC Code No.	Description	% of Total Exports to EBC's	PSTC Code No.	Description	% of Total Exports to EBC's	PSTC Code No.	Description	% of Total Exports to EBC's
2623 b	Animal hair, fine	0.01	8416 a	Apparel and clothing accessories	—	0223	Milk, cream, fresh	—
2927 a	Cut flower buds	—				2215 a	Linseed	—
5324 a	Tanning, extracts of vegetable origin	—				2631	Raw cotton, other than linters	22.21
6532 b	Woolen fabrics, woven	0.04				2893 b	Nonferrous metal	0.25
6577 a	Tapestries	0.11				2923	Vegetable material used for painting	—
6634	Worked mica	—				5122 a	Alcohols, phenols, glycerine	0.03
8611	Optical elements	—				6114		
8612	Spectacles and frames	0.10				6114	Leather	1.02
8613	Microscopes	—				6411 a	Newsprint paper	0.02
						6514	Cotton yarn, bleached	4.12
						6516 a	Yarn & thread of synthetic fiber	—
						6521	Cotton cloth, unbleached	7.54
						6522	Cotton cloth, bleached	7.39
						6569	Curtains, towels	1.27
						6576 b	Carpets other than knotted	0.11
						8510	Footwear	2.32
						8624	Photographic films, plates	—

Notes: a Exported in only one of the three years.

80

TABLE II-6

Pakistan's Imports from the EBC's by EBC Market Share, 1967/68-1969/70

31% and above			21-30%			11-20%		
PSTC Code No.	Description	% of Total Imports from EBC's	PSTC Code No.	Description	% of Total Imports from EBC's	PSTC Code No.	Description	% of Total Imports from EBC's
0422[b]	Rice, glazed or polished	3.21	2658[a]	Vegetable textile fiber	—	1221[a]	Cigars	—
0459[a]	Cereals, unmilled n.e.s.	—	2664[a]	Waste of synthetic or regenerated fiber	—	2662	Synthetic fiber	0.08
0612[b]	Refined sugar	5.19	2765	Quartz, mica, feldspar	—	2731[b]	Building stone	—
0615[a]	Molasses	—	3329	Pitch, resin, petroleum	0.21	2924	Plants, seeds, flowers	0.33
0619	Sugar & syrups	0.05	4229	Fixed vegetable oils n.e.s.	—	5122	Alcohols, phenols, glycerine	0.12
0620	Sugar confectionary	0.11	5142	Other metallic salts (I)	0.97	5125	Acids & derivatives	0.44
0741[b]	Tea	0.53	5310	Organic dyestuffs	2.46	5141	Metallic salts	0.16
1122[a]	Cider & fermented beers	—	5331	Coloring material	0.22	5416	Glycocides, glands, extracts	0.02
2515[a]	Pulp	—	5611	Nitrogenous fertilizer	6.70	6328	Articles of wood	0.02
2611[a]	Silkworm cocoons	—	5619[a]	Fertilizer n.e.s.	0.38	6514	Cotton yarn, bleached	0.06
2613[a]	Raw Silk	—	5714	Hunting ammunition	0.13	6517	Yarn of fiber	0.22
2655[a]	Manila fiber	—	6415	Machine-made paper	0.19	6561	Bags & sacks of textile	—
2663[b]	Regenerated fiber	0.09	6624	Ceramic bricks, tiles, pipes	0.08	6613[b]	Building stone	—
2714[a]	Natural polassic salt	—	6721	Puddled bars and pilings	—	6618	Material of asbestos	0.03
2732[b]	Gypsum, plaster, limestone	—	6781	Tubes of cast iron	0.39	6642[a]	Optical glass	—
2733[b]	Sand	—	6792	Steel casting	0.03	6645	Cast & rolled glass	—
2734[a]	Gravel & crushed stone	—	6841[a]	Aluminum and alloys	0.61	6646[a]	Bricks, tiles, & other material	—
2764	Asbestos	0.35	6895	Base metal	0.01	6647	Safety glass	0.01

(Continued)

TABLE II-6 (Continued)

	31% and above			21-30%			11-20%	
PSTC Code No.	Description	% of Total Imports from EBC's	PSTC Code No.	Description	% of Total Imports from EBC's	PSTC Code No.	Description	% of Total Imports from EBC's
2741	Sulphur	0.54	6931	Wire cable, ropes	0.57	6648	Sheet & plate glass	0.03
2831[a]	Ores & concentrate of copper	—	6981	Locksmith's ware	0.18	6651	Corboys, bottles, jars	0.24
2837[b]	Ores & concentrate of magnesium	—	7195	Powered tools n.e.s.	0.23	6665[b]	Household ware	—
2919	Material of animal origin	0.03	7151	Machine tools	1.69	6729	Blanks for tubes & pipes	0.15
2926	Bulbs & tubers, flowering	—	7221	Electric power machinery	4.26	6782	Seamless tubes and pipes	0.28
3214	Coal	7.01	7232	Electrical equipment	0.95	6783	Clinched tubes and pipes	0.45
3216	Lignite	—	7296	Electric mechanic hand tools	0.13	6861	Zinc & zinc alloys	0.24
3218	Coke & semicoke	1.41	7333	Trailers	0.16	6911	Finished structures of steel	2.31
3326	Mineral jelly & wakes	0.26	8122	Sinks and wash-basins	0.12	6923	Compressed gas cylinders	0.09
4216[b]	Sunflower seed oil	2.19	8415	Headgear	—	6932	Wire of iron	0.02
5127	Nitrogen-function compounds	0.79	8617	Medical instruments	0.19	6934[b]	Expanded metal	—
5149	Inorganic chemical products	0.29	8943	Nonmilitary arms	0.18	6960	Cutlery	0.05
5153	Compounds & mixtures n.e.s.	—	8944	Sporting goods	0.06	6983	Chains of iron	0.05
5711[a]	Propellant powders	—	8951	Office stationery of base metal	0.02	6989	Articles of metal	0.24
6411	Newsprint paper	—	8992	Brooms, brushes	0.04	7111	Steam boilers	0.64
6511	Thrown silk & silk yarn	0.13	8995	Toilet articles	0.07	7112	Boilerhouse plant	0.25
6513	Cotton yarn, unbleached	0.53				7118	Engines	0.11
6612	Cement	1.73				7125	Tractors	2.72
6631	Grinding wheels	0.15				7129	Agricultural machines n.e.s.	0.05

31% and above		% of Total Imports from EBC's	21-30%		% of Total Imports from EBC's	11-20%		% of Total Imports from EBC's
PSTC Code No.	Description		PSTC Code No.	Description		PSTC Code No.	Description	
6632	Abrasive cloth	0.12				7184	Mining machinery	4.67
6531[a]	Silk fabrics, woven	–				7193	Handling equipment	1.50
6637	Refractory products	0.07				7197	Ball & roller bearings	0.57
6643[a]	Drawn & blown glass	–				7199	Parts of machinery	1.61
6658	Articles made of glass	0.26				7295	Electrical instruments	0.38
6664	Porcelain	0.48				7299	Electrical goods	1.11
6712	Pig iron	3.14				8124	Lighting fixtures	0.08
6731	Wire rods	0.25				8210	Furniture	0.06
6880[a]	Uranium & thorium	–				8996[a]	Orthopedic appliances	–
6941	Nails, tacks, staples	0.15						
6951	Handtools for agriculture	0.07						
6952	Other tools for hand or machine	1.64						
6985	Pins & needles	0.15						
7316[a]	Railway & train maintenance cars	0.31						
7331	Bicycles	0.49						
7359	Ships & boats n.e.s.	1.02						
8642	Clocks & parts	0.80						
8918	Musical instruments	–						
8942	Children's toys	0.06						
8952[b]	Pens, pencils, fountain pens	0.17						
8972[a]	Imitation jewelry	0.01						

Notes: [a]Imported in only one of the three years.
[b]Imported in only two of the three years.

TABLE II-7

EBC's Share of East Pakistan's Major Exports, 1967/68-1969/70
(thousand rupees)

PSTC Code No.	Description	Exports to the World[a]	% of Exports to the World	Exports to the EBC's[b]	% of Exports to the EBC's	Exports to EBC's as % of Exports to World	Exports to EBC's taken by:					
							China		Russia		East Europe	
							Amount	%	Amount	%	Amount	%
2640	Jute raw	750,645.2	48.09	156,355.0	85.84	20.83	68,519.8	42.82	22,848.3	14.61	64,986.9	42.57
6114	Leather	23,072.7	1.48	1,522.5	0.84	6.60	—	—	540.4	35.50	982.0	64.50
6119	Leather, skins	35,957.8	2.30	5,465.0	3.00	15.20	—	—	1,436.0	26.28	4,029.0	73.72
6534	Jute fabrics	398,136.2	25.50	4,653.6	2.55	1.17	135.7	2.92	10.4	0.22	4,522.7	97.19
6561	Bags & sacks of textile	264,330.7	16.94	9,072.9	4.98	3.43	556.8	6.14	299.9	3.31	7,866.0	86.70

Notes: [a] 1 percent and above of all exports to the world in each of the three years.
[b] Exports to Mongolia are included in EBC total.

TABLE II-8

EBC's Share of East Pakistan's Major Imports, 1967/68-1969/70
(thousand rupees)

PSTC Code No.	Description	Imports from the World*	% of Imports from the World	Imports from the EBC's	% of Imports from EBC's	Imports from EBC's as % of Imports from World	Imports from EBC's supplied by:					
							China		Russia		East Europe	
							Amount	%	Amount	%	Amount	%
3214	Coal	36,518.3	2.21	33,974.2	16.04	93.03	16,869.3	49.65	–	–	17,104.8	50.35
5417	Medicaments	22,192.0	1.34	1,979.1	0.93	8.92	558.6	28.23	140.0	7.07	1,280.5	64.70
5611	Nitrogenous fertilizers	37,920.7	2.29	6,724.1	3.18	17.73	1.7	0.03	145.2	2.16	6,577.2	97.82
5992	Insecticides	47,370.6	2.86	2,989.5	1.42	6.35	233.1	8.35	–	–	2,758.4	91.65
6612	Cement	19,928.3	1.20	9,350.8	4.42	46.92	4,995.3	53.42	132.1	14.12	3,034.9	32.46
6725	Blooms, billets	46,687.2	2.82	1,480.3	0.70	3.17	1,480.3	100.00	–	–	–	–
6741	Universal heavy plates	59,250.8	3.58	609.2	0.29	1.03	357.5	58.68	0.1	0.01	251.7	41.31
6911	Finished structures of steel	32,945.9	1.99	10,866.8	5.13	32.98	2.6	0.02	2,538.5	23.36	8,325.6	76.62
7115	Internal combustion engines	39,376.5	2.38	3,233.4	1.53	8.21	8.4	0.26	1,132.0	35.01	2,092.9	64.73
7171	Textile machines	118,997.3	7.19	1,379.8	0.65	1.16	279.6	20.26	1,098.5	79.61	1.7	0.12
7193	Mechanical handling equipment	19,893.3	1.20	4,300.6	2.03	21.62	12.7	0.30	1,497.1	34.81	2,803.5	65.19
7198	Machinery	33,125.9	2.00	2,561.8	1.21	7.73	57.2	2.23	1,558.0	60.82	946.6	36.95
7199	Machinery parts	32,125.3	1.94	4,115.5	1.66	12.81	157.5	3.83	1,701.2	41.34	2,756.8	54.84
7221	Electric power machinery	37,624.4	2.27	10,293.4	4.86	27.36	70.8	0.69	878.4	8.53	9,344.1	90.78
7222	Switchgear	22,128.6	1.34	8,673.4	4.10	39.20	197.2	2.27	49.2	0.57	8,427.0	97.16

Note: * 1 percent and above of all imports from the world in each of the three years.

TABLE II-9

East Pakistan's Exports to the EBC's by EBC Market Share, 1967/68-1969/70

76-100%			51-75%			26-50%		
PSTC Code No.	Description	% of Total Exports to EBC's	PSTC Code No.	Description	% of Total Exports to EBC's	PSTC Code No.	Description	% of Total Exports to EBC's
5122[a]	Alcohols, phenols, glycerine	0.06	6576[b]	Carpets other than knotted	0.25	6411[a]	Newsprint paper	0.05
7222[a]	Switch-gear	—				6578[a]	Mats, matting	0.01
8613[a]	Microscopes	—						
8993	Candles, matches	—						

Notes: [a]Exported in only one of the three years.
[b]Exported in only two of the three years.

TABLE II-10
East Pakistan's Imports from the EBC's by EBC Market Share, 1967/68-1969/70

	31% and above			21%-30%			11-20%	
PSTC Code No.	Description	% of Total Imports from EBC's	PSTC Code No.	Description	% of Total Imports from EBC's	PSTC Code No.	Description	% of Total Imports from EBC's
0422[b]	Rice, glazed or polished	7.83	0722	Cocoa powder	–	0138	Other preserved meat	–
0459	Cereals, unmilled n.e.s.	–	0752	Spices	0.08			
0612	Refined sugar	1.48	3326	Mineral jelly & waxes	0.20	1121	Wine & fresh grapes	–
0619	Sugar & syrups	0.09	5127	Nitrogen-function compounds	0.45	1222	Cigarettes	0.02
0741[b]	Tea	1.29				2218	Oilseeds, nuts, kernels	0.04
2633	Cotton waste	–	5135	Compounds and mixtures n.e.s.	–	2769	Mineral, crude n.e.s.	–
2731[a]	Building stone	–	5310	Organic dyestuffs	1.59			
2732[a]	Gypsum, plaster, limestone	–	5530[b]	Cosmetics	–	3325	Lubricating oil & grease	0.31
2733	Sand	–	5714	Hunting ammunition	0.04	5122	Alcohols, phenols, glycerine	0.09
2741	Sulphur	0.51	6412	Other printing papers	0.23	5125	Acid & derivatives	0.18
2765	Quartz, mica, feldspar	–	6517	Yarn of fiber	0.03	5128	Organic & inorganic compounds	–
2924	Plants, seeds, flowers	0.51	6651	Corboys, bottles, jars	0.33	5132	Chemical elements n.e.s.	0.15
3214	Coal	15.18	6658	Articles made of glass	0.14	5141	Metallic salt	0.21
3218[b]	Coke, semicoke	0.51	6665[b]	Household ware	–	5325[b]	Tannic acids	–
3323	Distillate fuels	0.09	6941	Nails, tacks, staples	0.08	5416	Glycosides, glands, & extracts	0.06
4229	Fixed vegetable oils n.e.s.	–	6989	Articles of metal	0.16	5611	Nitrogenous fertilizer	3.01
5134[b]	Helogen, sulphur compounds	–	7111	Steam boilers	1.54	6291	Rubber tires	0.16
5142	Other metallic salts (I)	1.25	7125	Tractors	0.84	6411	Newsprint paper	–
5149	Inorganic chemical products	0.08	7193	Handling equipment	1.92	6416	Fiber board	0.01
5713[a]	Pyrotechnical articles	–	7197	Ball & roller bearings	0.48	6419	Paper & paperboard	0.19
6415	Machine-made paper	0.29	7221	Electric power machinery	4.60	6423	Exercise books	–
6421	Paper bags & paperboard	0.11	7323	Lorries & trucks	0.36	6514	Cotton yarn, bleached	0.16
6511	Thrown silk, silk yarn	–	7324	Special lorries	0.34	6521	Cotton cloth, unbleached	–
6513	Cotton yarn, unbleached	1.29	8122	Sinks & wash basins	0.05	6551	Felts & felt articles	0.03
6515	Yarn & thread of flax, etc.	–	8922	Newspapers & periodicals	0.01	6635[a]	Mineral insulating	0.01
6535	Fabrics woven of synthetic fiber	–	8959[b]	Office & stationery supplies	0.05	6649	Glass n.e.s.	0.04
6540[a]	Tulle, lace & other small ware	–	8999	Other manufactured articles	0.07	6770	Steel wire	0.19
6612	Cement	4.18				6785	Tube and pipe fittings	0.55
6624[b]	Ceramic bricks, tiles, pipes	0.03				6822	Copper & alloys, worked	0.24
6632	Abrasive cloth	0.13				6895	Base metal	–
6637[b]	Refractory products	0.02				6923	Compressed gas cylinders	0.04
6642	Optical glass	–				6934[b]	Expanded metal	–
6643[a]	Drawn & blown glass	–				6942	Nuts, bolts	0.40
6644[b]	Cast, rolled, drawn glass	–				6960	Cutlery	0.02
6646	Bricks, tiles of other material	–				7141	Typewriters	0.05
6652	Glass tableware	0.01				7149	Office machinery	0.02
6664	Porcelain	0.10				7199	Parts of machinery	1.84
6712	Pig iron	4.28				7291	Batteries & accumulators	0.17
6731	Wire rods	0.50				7292	Electric lamps	0.06
6841[a]	Aluminum & alloys	0.76				7359	Ships & boats n.e.s.	0.26
						8123	Sinks & wash basins of steel iron	0.02
						8124	Lighting fixtures	1.08
						8210	Furniture	0.02

(Continued)

87

TABLE II-10 (Continued)

31% and above		% of Total Imports from EBC's	21%-30%		% of Total Imports from EBC's	11-20%		% of Total Imports from EBC's
PSTC Code No.	Description		PSTC Code No.	Description		PSTC Code No.	Description	
6911	Finished struc-tures of steel	4.86				6813	Binoculars	0.01
6912[b]	Finished struc-tures of aluminum	0.01				8911	Phonographs	0.01
6931	Wire, cable, ropes	0.55				8929	Printed matters	0.06
6951	Hand tools of agriculture	0.10				8943	Nonmilitary arms	0.06
6952	Other tools for hand or machine	1.14						
6981	Locksmith's ware	0.20						
6982	Safes, etc.	–						
6985	Pins & needles	0.15						
7143	Statistical machines	0.03						
7151	Machine tools	1.59						
7152	Metal working machinery	0.24						
7184	Mining machinery	2.45						
7195	Powered tools n.e.s.	0.44						
7222	Switch-gear	3.88						
7231	Insulated wire & cables	1.39						
7232	Electrical equipment	1.43						
7261	Electrical medical apparatus	0.12						
7295	Electrical instru-ments	0.31						
7296	Electrical mechan-ical hand tools	0.07						
7299	Electrical goods	2.17						
7315[b]	Railway & train passenger cars	0.40						
7316	Railway & train maintenance cars	0.75						
7331	Bicycles	0.90						
7333	Trailers	0.28						
8617	Medical instru-ments	0.33						
8618	Meters, nonelectric	0.01						
8619	Measuring, con-trolling & scien-tific instruments	3.08						
8642	Clocks & parts	0.04						
8914	Pianos	–						
8919	Parts of musical instruments	–						
8942	Children's toys	0.06						
8945[a]	Fairground equipment	–						
8951	Office stationery of base metal	0.02						
8952[b]	Pens, pencils, fountain pens	0.16						
8971	Jewelry, gold, silver, plated	–						
8972	Imitation jewelry	0.04						
8992	Brooms, brushes	0.02						
8995	Toilet articles	0.03						
8996[a]	Orthopedic appliances	–						

Notes: [a]Imported in only one of the three years.
[b]Imported in only two of the three years.

TABLE II-11

EBC's Share of West Pakistan's Major Exports, 1967/68-1969/70

(thousand rupees)

| PSTC Code No. | Description | Exports to the World[a] | % of Total Exports to the World | Exports to the EBC's[b] | % of Total Exports to EBC's | Exports to EBC's as % of Exports to World | Exports to EBC's taken by: | | | | | |
| | | | | | | | China | | Russia | | East Europe | |
							Amount	%	Amount	%	Amount	%
0313	Molluscs, crustacea	26,948.2	2.44	11.7	0.01	0.40	0.7	5.79	1.6	13.34	9.7	80.88
0422	Rice, glazed or polished	132,816.3	8.04	24,387.1	8.96	18.36	—	—	20,386.7	83.60	4,001.5	16.49
2622	Raw wool	34,859.1	2.11	4,722.3	1.74	13.55	—	—	4,005.7	84.83	814.4	17.25
2631	Raw cotton other than linters	331,829.5	20.10	100,884.4	37.07	30.40	43,210.4	42.83	8,065.9	8.00	49,608.1	49.17
6113	Calf leather	26,921.9	1.63	787.4	2.29	2.92	—	—	—	—	787.3	100.00
6119	Leather, skins	66,110.6	4.00	8,801.8	3.23	13.31	—	—	945.6	10.74	8,089.6	91.91
6513	Cotton yarn, unbleached	155,630.6	9.43	10,387.2	3.82	6.68	4,020.6	38.68	16.4	0.16	6,357.0	61.61
6514	Cotton yarn, bleached	68,696.9	4.16	17,877.1	6.57	26.02	348.2	1.95	1,478.6	8.27	16,050.2	89.78
6521	Cotton cloth, unbleached	129,336.8	7.83	33,128.5	12.17	25.61	—	—	53.5	0.16	33,073.0	99.84
6522	Cotton cloth, bleached	78,014.6	4.73	32,583.7	11.97	41.77	67.7	0.21	13,408.0	41.15	19,107.9	58.64
6575	Knotted carpets, rugs	41,288.1	2.50	2,117.2	0.78	5.13	—	—	18.5	0.87	2,098.7	99.13
8510	Footwear	26,601.8	1.61	10,515.1	3.86	39.54	—	—	7,046.3	67.01	3,468.8	32.99
8944	Sporting goods	26,547.4	1.61	238.4	0.09	0.90	0.5	0.21	25.3	10.62	212.6	89.17

Notes: [a]1 percent and above all exports to the world in each of the three years.
[b]Exports to Mongolia are included in the EBC total.

TABLE II-12

EBC's Share of West Pakistan's Major Imports, 1967/68-1969/70
(thousand rupees)

PSTC Code No.	Description	Imports from the World*	% of total Imports from the World	Imports from the EBC's	% of total Imports from EBC's	Imports from EBC's as % of Imports from World	Imports from EBC's Supplied by:					
							China		Russia		East Europe	
							Amount	%	Amount	%	Amount	%
5417	Medicaments	38,533.4	1.20	3,102.3	0.96	8.05	876.9	28.26	185.6	5.98	2,039.9	65.75
5611	Nitrogenous fertilizer	137,381.0	4.27	29,843.5	9.26	21.72	2.3	0.01	13,999.3	46.91	15,842.0	53.08
6725	Blooms, billets	76,317.1	2.37	8,817.4	2.74	11.55	117.2	1.33	8,647.9	98.08	52.3	0.59
6741	Universal heavy plates	84,465.4	2.62	2,044.9	0.63	2.42	110.2	5.39	21.9	1.07	1,912.8	93.54
6911	Finished structures of steel	39,051.4	1.21	1,758.6	0.55	4.50	65.3	3.72	6.2	0.35	1,687.1	95.93
7125	Tractors	76,582.2	2.38	12,733.9	3.95	16.63	-	-	11,472.8	90.10	1,135.5	8.92
7171	Textile machines	130,670.2	4.06	6,992.2	2.17	5.35	2,055.5	29.40	756.2	10.81	4,180.5	59.79
7184	Construction & mining machinery	111,599.7	3.47	20,008.1	6.21	17.93	32.7	0.16	13,320.8	66.58	6,654.7	33.26
7199	Machinery parts	46,776.8	1.45	4,673.7	1.45	9.99	217.9	4.66	2,158.6	46.19	2,297.2	49.15
7221	Electric power machinery	56,822.3	1.76	12,968.1	4.02	22.82	473.8	3.65	396.4	3.06	12,097.9	93.29
7222	Switchgear	43,410.8	1.35	1,469.8	0.46	3.39	332.0	22.59	10.3	0.70	1,127.4	76.71
7321	Passenger motorcars	42,921.4	1.33	337.0	0.10	0.79	46.3	13.75	204.4	60.64	86.3	25.61

TABLE II-13

West Pakistan's Exports to the EBC's by EBC Market Share, 1967/68-1969/70

76-100%			51-75%			26-50%		
PSTC Code No.	Description	% of Total Exports to EBC's	PSTC Code No.	Description	% of Total Exports to EBC's	PSTC Code No.	Description	% of Total Exports to EBC's
2623[b]	Animal hair, fine	0.02	8416[a]	Apparel & clothing accessories	–	0223[b]	Milk, cream, fresh	–
2927[a]	Cut flower buds	–	8510	Footwear	3.86	2215[a]	Linseed	–
5324[a]	Tanning, extracts of vegetables	–				2631	Raw cotton, other than linters	37.07
6532[b]	Woolen fabrics, woven	0.07				2839	Nonferrous metal	0.41
6577[a]	Tapestries	0.19				2923[a]	Vegetable material used for painting	0.05
6634[a]	Worked mica	–				6114[b]	Leather	1.15
8611	Optical elements	–				6514	Cotton yarn, bleached	6.57
8612[b]	Spectacles and frames	0.23				6516[a]	Yarn & thread of synthetic fiber	–
8614[a]	Photographic cameras	0.17				6521	Cotton cloth, unbleached	12.17
						6522	Cotton cloth, bleached	11.97
						6569	Curtains, towels	2.13
						8624	Photographic film, plates	–

Notes: [a]Exported in only one of the three years.
[b]Exported in only two of the three years.

TABLE II-14

West Pakistan's Imports from the EBC's by EBC Market Share, 1967/68-1969/70

31% and above			21-30%			11-20%		
PSTC Code No.	Description	% of Total Imports from EBC's	PSTC Code No.	Description	% of Total Imports from EBC's	PSTC Code No.	Description	% of Total Imports from EBC's
0422	Rice, glazed or polished	–	2658	Vegetable textile fiber	0.01	0619	Sugar & syrups	0.03
0611	Raw sugar, beet, cane	–	2662	Synthetic fiber	0.14	1221[a]	Cigars	–
0612	Refined sugar	7.77	2664[b]	Waste of synthetic & regenerated fiber	–	2762	Clay	0.09
0615[a]	Molasses	–				5122	Alcohols, phenols, glycerine	0.14
0620	Sugar confectionery	0.19	3326	Mineral jelly & waxes	0.15	5124	Aldehyde, ketone, etc.	0.06
1122	Cider & fermented beverages	–	4229	Fixed vegetable oils n.e.s.	–	5125	Acids & derivatives	0.62
2431	Railway sleepers	2.03	5310	Organic dyestuffs	3.07	5131	Oxygen, nitrogen	0.02
2515	Pulp	–	5331	Coloring material	0.33	5141	Metallic salts	0.12
2611	Silkworm cocoons	–	5611	Nitrogenous fertilizer	9.26	5142	Other metallic salts (I)	0.77
2613	Raw silk	–	5619[a]	Fertilizer n.e.s.	0.64	5143	Other metallic salts (II)	0.10
2655	Manila fiber	–	5714	Hunting ammunition	0.20	5214[b]	Oils of other products	0.01
2663[b]	Regenerated fiber	0.15	6327[b]	Wood of domestic use	–	5413[b]	Penicillin & antibiotics	0.25
2714[a]	Natural potassic salt	–	6328	Articles of wood	0.03	5416	Glycocides, glands	0.02
2732	Gypsum, plaster, limestone	–	6561	Bags & sacks of textile	–	6415	Machine-made paper	0.17
2734[a]	Gravel & crushed stone	–	6618	Material of asbestos	0.06	6517	Yarn of fiber	0.35
2741	Sulphur	0.32	6637	Refraction products	0.10	6575	Carpets, rugs	–
2764	Asbestos	0.59	6658	Articles made of glass	0.26	6612	Cement	0.02
2831	Ores & concentrates of copper	–	6782	Seamless tubes & pipes	0.40	6624	Ceramic bricks, tiles, pipes	0.10
2837	Ores & concentrates of manganese	–	6783	Clinched tubes & pipes	0.76	6647	Safety glass	0.02
2919	Materials of animal origin	0.05	6792	Steel casting	0.05	6648	Sheet or plate glass	0.04
2926[a]	Bulbs & tubers, flowering	–	6951	Hand tools for agriculture	0.05	6729	Blanks for tubes & pipes	0.23
3214	Coal	1.34	6981	Locksmith's ware	0.17	6923	Compressed gas cylinders	0.13
3216[a]	Lignite	0.01	6985	Pins & needles	0.13	6931	Wirecables, ropes	0.59
3218	Coke, semicoke	2.03	7129	Agricultural machines n.e.s.	0.08	6932	Wire of iron	0.03
3329	Pitch, resin, petroleum	0.33	7151	Machine tools	1.75	6934[b]	Expanded metal	–
4216[b]	Sunflower seed oil	3.70	7195	Powered tools n.e.s.	0.29	6960	Cutlery	0.07
5127	Nitrogen-function compounds	1.02	7221	Electric power machinery	3.92	6861	Zinc & zinc alloys	0.36
						6983	Chains of iron	0.07

31% and above		% of Total Imports from EBC's	21-30%		% of Total Imports from EBC's	11-20%		% of Total Imports from EBC's
PSTC Code No.	Description		PSTC Code No.	Description		PSTC Code No.	Description	
5149	Inorganic chemical products	0.44	8943	Nonmilitary arms	0.26	6989	Articles of metal	0.29
5153	Compounds and mixtures n.e.s.	—	8951	Office stationery of base metal	0.02	7125	Tractors	3.95
5711[a]	Propellent powders	—	8952	Pens, pencils & fountain pens	0.13	7184	Mining machinery	6.21
6411	Newsprint paper	—	8959[b]	Other office & stationery supplies	0.05	7197	Ball & roller bearings	0.64
6511	Thrown silk & silk yarn	0.21	8995	Toilet articles	0.11	7199	Parts of machinery	1.45
6613[a]	Building stone	—				7292	Electric pumps	0.15
6631	Grinding wheels	0.21				7295	Electrical instruments	0.42
6632	Abrasive cloth	0.12				7328	Bodies, chassis, etc.	0.95
6645	Cast & rolled glass	0.01				8122	Sinks, washbasins	0.17
6664	Porcelain	0.75				8124	Lighting fixtures	0.81
6712	Pig iron	2.35				8210	Furniture	0.09
6721[a]	Puddled bars and pilings	0.02				8992	Brooms and brushes	0.06
6781[b]	Tubes of cast iron	0.66						
6880[a]	Uranium & thorium	0.03						
6895	Base metal	0.02						
6941	Nails, tacks, & staples	0.20						
6952	Other tools for hand or machine	1.93						
7112	Boilerhouse plant	0.27						
7113	Engines	0.18						
7173	Sewing machines	0.55						
7296	Electric mechanical hand tools	0.17						
7331	Bicycles	0.20						
7359	Ships and boats n.e.s.	1.51						
8415[b]	Headgear	—						
8642	Clocks & parts	0.10						
8918	Musical instruments	—						
8942	Children's toys	0.07						
8944	Sporting goods	0.08						
8972	Imitation jewelry	0.04						

Notes: [a]Imported in only one of the three years.
[b]Imported in only two of the three years.

TABLE II-15

Structure of Pakistan's Exports to the EBC's and to the World, 1960/61-1969/70

	1960/61			1961/62			1962/63			1963/64			1964/65		
	Pak.	E.P.	W.P.	Pak.	E.P.	W.P.	Pak.	E.P.	W.P.	Pak.	E.P.	W.P.	Pak.	E.P.	W.P.
Number of items providing 1 percent or more of total exports to:															
World	8	4	8	7	4	10	7	4	8	14	5	14	13	2	11
EBC's	4	3	1	2	1	4	2	1	2	5	3	3	6	3	6
Russia	3	2	1	2	1	4	2	1	6	2	1	3	2	1	3
E. Europe	1	4	1	1	1	1	2	2	5	4	4	2	6	2	10
China	3	3	1	5	5	2	2	1	1	4	2	3	5	2	3
Proportion of total exports contributed by top three commodities exported to:															
World	66	92	53	78	96	78	61	88	64	63	89	58	54	89	42
EBC's	97	98	100	98	99	97	99	100	99	95	98	97	91	98	92
Russia	98	99	99	100	100	93	100	100	94	100	100	98	100	100	100
E. Europe	99	95	99	98	100	98	99	100	93	96	100	98	68	100	85
China	98	99	100	93	100	99	100	100	100	98	100	98	95	100	99
Section 8 commodities as a proportion of total exports to:															
World	0.9	0.4	3.1	1.6	0.13	7.2	1.5	0.03	3.4	2.2	–	5.0	2.0	0.03	4.3
EBC's	0.004	–	0.01	0.3	–	0.3	0.2	–	0.9	0.02	–	0.03	0.1	–	0.3
Russia	–	–	–	1.5	–	88.9	0.08	–	4.7	–	–	–	–	–	–
E. Europe	0.006	–	0.006	0.007	–	0.007	0.6	–	1.0	0.1	–	0.4	0.3	–	1.9
China	–	–	–	0.32	0.31	0.36	–	–	–	–	–	–	0.2	–	0.4

	1965/66			1966/67			1967/68			1968/69			1969/70		
	Pak.	E.P.	W.P.	Pak.	E.P.	W.P.	Pak.	E.P.	W.P.	Pak.	E.P.	W.P.	Pak.	E.P.	W.P.
Number of items providing 1 percent or more of total exports to:															
World	10	5	13	11	6	13	13	6	16	17	10	14	12	4	18
EBC's	8	3	5	7	3	7	9	3	9	12	6	10	14	5	13
Russia	6	2	4	7	3	5	9	1	7	10	4	8	10	2	10
E. Europe	9	2	7	9	2	9	12	5	7	10	5	8	12	5	12
China	5	3	2	5	3	2	3	1	2	4	1	3	4	2	3
Proportion of total exports contributed by top three commodities exported to:															
World	59	93	41	51	91	41	49	91	44	45	89	30	47	91	27
EBC's	76	99	84	85	99	88	74	97	52	77	92	70	60	92	55
Russia	82	99	64	85	100	90	73	100	84	66	96	72	67	100	61
E. Europe	85	100	79	84	98	71	61	93	67	72	96	69	50	89	51
China	87	99	98	95	98	96	100	100	100	95	100	99	97	100	99
Section 8 commodities as a proportion of total exports to:															
World	3.9	0.3	8.8	2.2	–	5.0	3.0	0.02	5.6	3.9	0.1	7.3	3.8	0.08	8.00
EBC's	0.5	–	1.0	1.3	–	2.4	3.8	–	6.8	3.6	–	5.4	2.65	–	4.68
Russia	0.7	–	1.0	4.1	–	5.0	12.3	–	15.7	7.8	–	12.0	0	–	–
E. Europe	0.8	–	2.6	0.02	–	0.04	2.9	–	4.2	2.4	–	4.4	0.45	–	0.62
China	0.3	–	0.6	0.2	–	0.6	–	–	–	–	–	–	–	–	–

95

TABLE II-16

Weighted Average Unit Prices of Pakistan's Exports to the EBC's
as a Percentage of Exports to the World,
1960/61-1969/70

PSTC section	1960/61	1961/62	1962/63	1963/64	1964/65	1965/66	1966/67	1967/68	1968/69	1969/70	Average 1960/61 -1969/70
0	0.07	0.02	0.05	–	1.36	12.07	16.63	9.25	7.27	2.43	4.92
1	–	–	–	–	–	–	–	–	–	0.42	0.04
2	102.68	102.31	135.76	96.95	95.75	61.05	72.90	82.72	64.36	52.67	86.72
6	4.68	5.43	0.79	5.93	17.86	19.56	11.81	23.16	31.24	46.83	16.73
8	0.01	1.10	0.34	0.05	0.41	0.70	2.23	5.04	5.50	6.52	2.19
All exports	107.44	108.86	136.94	102.93	115.38	93.38	103.57	120.17	108.37	108.77	110.60

Unit Prices of Pakistan's Exports to the EBC's and the World, 1960/61
(Rs per unit)

Code (1)	Commodity (2)	World (3)	EBC's (4)	East Europe (5)	U.S.S.R. (6)	China (7)	EBC Price as % of World (8) $\frac{(4)}{(3)}$ x100	% Weight in EBC Section Total (9)	Adjusted EBC Price as % of World: by Intra-section Weight (10)
0130901	Sausage casing	375.72	892.18	892.18	–	–	237.46	98.07	237.46
Section 0								98.07	237.46
2630109	Raw cotton n.e.s.	2,632.89	2,508.51	2,658.14	–	2,507.58	95.26	10.45	30.10
2640105	Jute cuttings	868.30	1,202.83	1,202.83	–	–	138.53	0.35	1.47
2640109	Jute n.e.s.	1,797.60	2,068.16	1,951.42	2,252.68	2,354.97	115.05	22.27	77.48
Section 2								33.07	109.05
6110101	Crust and tanned leather	267.47	365.69	365.69	–	–	136.72	0.50	2.88
6110105	Crust tanned leather n.e.s.	256.03	426.38	426.38	–	–	166.54	0.26	1.82
6410100	Newsprint paper	31.05	30.90	–	30.90	–	99.52	0.61	2.56
6510429	Cotton and yarn n. e. s.	1.91	1.53	–	–	1.53	80.10	0.93	3.14
6530402	Hessian gunny-cloth	2.27	2.38	–	–	2.38	104.85	0.36	1.59
6560101	Jute gunny bags	1,457.68	1,131.96	1,896.72	–	1,125.99	77.65	21.09	68.95
Section 6								23.75	80.94
8991403	Badminton rackets	15.34	22.65	22.65	–	–	147.65	16.29	147.65
Section 8								16.29	147.65

TABLE II-18

Unit Prices of Pakistan's Exports to the EBC's and the World, 1961/62
(Rs per unit)

Code (1)	Commodity (2)	World (3)	EBC's (4)	East Europe (5)	U.S.S.R. (6)	China (7)	EBC Price as % of World (4x100/(3)) (8)	% Weight in EBC Section Total (9)	Adjusted EBC Price as % of World: by Intrasection Weight (10)
0130901	Sausage casing	926.72	1,156.00	1,304.00	—	1,600.00	124.74	99.88	124.74
Section 0								99.88	124.74
2630109	Raw cotton n.e.s.	2,542.14	3,194.99	2,743.43	—	3,254.20	125.68	8.28	10.44
2630319	Cotton waste	62.32	85.09	—	85.09	—	136.54	0.02	0.03
2640105	Jute cuttings	676.01	853.32	855.94	709.96	—	126.23	1.51	1.91
2640109	Jute n.e.s.	1,316.87	1,345.11	1,336.91	1,387.49	1,257.61	102.14	89.89	92.09
Section 2								99.70	104.47
6410100	Newsprint paper	5.01	30.32	—	—	30.32	605.19	26.42	246.67
6530402	Jute hessian cloth	1,029.40	1,902.93	2,025.29	—	1,825.88	184.86	4.82	13.75
6530409	Fabrics of jute	1,243.86	2,021.14	2,021.14	—	—	162.49	4.07	10.20
6550601	Cordage twine, rope, etc., of jute	70.17	59.85	—	—	59.85	85.29	1.89	2.49
6560101	Jute gunny bags	1,376.52	1,553.39	1,451.61	—	1,565.10	112.85	27.62	48.09
Section 6								64.82	321.20
8510201	Footwear	77.99	313.13	—	313.13	—	401.50	50.42	242.26
8510209	Footwear, leather	73.14	187.01	—	187.26	—	255.69	31.85	97.46
8991414	Hockey sticks	46.85	60.46	60.46	—	—	129.05	0.80	1.24
8991418	Tennis rackets	24.80	71.40	—	—	71.40	287.90	0.49	1.69

TABLE II-19

Unit Prices of Pakistan's Exports to the EBC's and the World, 1962/63

Code (1)	Commodity (2)	World (3)	EBC's (4)	East Europe (5)	U.S.S.R. (6)	China (7)	EBC Price as % of World = (8) = (4) x 100 (3)	% Weight in EBC Section Total (9)	Adjusted EBC Price as % of World: by intra-section weight (10)
0420209	Rice, not in the husk n.e.s.	940.97	832.85	—	—	832.85	88.51	98.02	86.76
0480401	Biscuits	113.31	155.25	—	—	155.25	137.01	1.98	2.71
Section 0								100.00	89.47
2630109	Raw cotton n.e.s.	2,382.77	2,503.81	—	—	2,503.81	105.08	25.42	26.81
2630319	Cotton waste	61.52	92.25	—	—	92.25	149.95	0.30	0.45
2640105	Jute cuttings	504.64	621.73	621.74	—	—	123.20	0.63	0.78
2640109	Jute n.e.s.	803.53	1,192.79	1,162.53	1,248.73	1,201.62	148.44	73.27	109.18
Section 2								99.62	137.22
6530402	Jute hessian cloth	901.28	1,782.18	1,767.40	—	1,795.14	197.74	27.17	58.34
6530409	Fabrics of jute	1,332.35	1,232.08	1,232.08	—	—	92.47	64.92	65.19
Section 6								92.09	123.53
8510101	All-leather slippers	68.17	120.42	120.42	—	—	176.65	9.20	17.59
8510209	Footwear, leather	83.67	109.05	109.05	—	—	130.33	27.57	38.89
8510909	Footwear n. e. s. and parts	116.83	207.49	207.49	—	—	177.60	24.16	46.44
8630109	Cinema films, exposed	0.26	0.22	0.22	—	—	84.62	6.36	5.83
8991411	Footballs, complete	54.19	76.14	76.14	—	—	140.51	25.10	38.17
Section 8								92.39	146.92

TABLE II-20

Unit Prices of Pakistan's Exports to the EBC's and the World, 1963/64
(Rs per unit)

Code (1)	Commodity (2)	World (3)	EBC's (4)	East Europe (5)	U.S.S.R. (6)	China (7)	EBC Price as % of World $=\frac{(4)}{(3)} \times 100$ (8)	% Weight in EBC Section Total (9)	Adjusted EBC Price as % of World: Intrasection Weight (10)
263199	Raw cotton n. e. s.	2,100.29	2,550.95	2,550.95	–	–	121.46	8.84	21.06
264003	Jute cuttings	552.90	593.35	588.21	–	664.41	107.32	0.42	0.88
264004	Jute waste	579.40	559.58	559.58	–	–	96.58	0.004	0.01
264005	Mesta	726.84	755.79	755.78	–	755.86	103.98	0.21	0.43
264006	Mesta cuttings	486.58	538.92	–	–	538.92	110.76	0.01	0.02
264099	Jute n.e.s.	1,113.93	1,118.82	1,110.52	1,441.59	1,045.12	100.44	41.50	81.76
Section 2								50.98	104.08
611901	Leather, sheepskin	426.51	316.10	316.10	–	–	74.11	0.08	0.16
611902	Leather, lambskin	363.69	400.49	400.49	–	–	110.12	0.40	1.18
611903	Leather, goatskin	400.20	300.14	300.14	–	–	75.00	0.06	0.12
611912	Leather, crome	250.48	142.15	–	–	142.15	56.75	0.01	0.02
611999	Leather n.e.s.	281.18	236.54	203.22	–	415.65	84.12	0.04	0.09
651302	Cotton yarn, unbleached 21-34	1.69	1.53	–	–	1.53	90.53	27.40	66.36
651303	Cotton yarn, unbleached 35-47	2.10	2.48	–	–	2.48	118.10	0.95	3.00
651399	Cotton yarn, unbleached n. e. s.	1.61	1.74	–	–	1.74	108.07	6.95	20.0
651499	Cotton yarn and twist n. e. s.	1.88	6.36	–	–	6.36	338.30	1.44	13.03
656101	Jute gunny bags	1,146.83	1,810.80	–	–	1,610.80	157.90	0.05	0.2
Section 6								37.38	104.2
861799	Medical instruments	2.22	8.31	8.31	–	–	374.32	38.60	156.2
891813	Vellum drum heads	7.78	15.47	–	–	15.47	198.84	22.18	47.7
891899	Musical instruments	2.13	1.46	1.46	–	–	68.54	5.43	4.0
894411	Footballs, complete	65.13	83.00	83.00	–	–	127.44	0.46	0.6
894418	Tennis rackets	22.67	54.64	54.64	–	–	241.02	6.78	17.6
894422	Volley balls, complete	61.98	56.00	–	–	56.00	90.35	0.10	0.1
894499	Sports goods, n. e. s.	31.29	53.78	35.00	–	54.49	171.88	5.48	10.1
895999	Office supplies n.e.s.	2.50	2.75	–	1.41	6.75	110.00	6.45	7.4
899999	Manufactured n.e.s.	14.65	15.43	–	15.43	–	105.32	6.97	7.9
Section 8								92.45	254.0

TABLE II-21

Unit Prices of Pakistan's Exports to the EBC's and the World, 1964/65
(Rs per unit)

Code (1)	Commodity (2)	World (3)	EBC's (4)	East Europe (5)	U.S.S.R. (6)	China (7)	EBC Price as % of World $= \frac{(4)}{(3)} \times 100$ (8)	% Weight in EBC Section Total (9)	Adjusted EBC Price as % of World: by Intrasection Weight (10)
42201	Rice, fine quality	1,102.07	1,104.75	1,104.75	–	–	100.24	87.62	88.38
42202	Rice, medium quality	720.46	778.95	778.95	–	–	108.12	4.94	5.37
31301	Cake, cotton seed	18.57	21.10	21.10	–	–	113.62	4.33	4.95
31302	Cake, rape seed	13.35	13.41	13.41	–	–	100.45	2.41	2.44
41399	Cake, oil seed n.e.s.	14.96	10.00	–	–	10.00	66.84	0.08	0.05
Section 0								99.38	101.19
2101	Raw wool, greasy	2.63	2.00	2.00	–	–	76.05	0.45	0.34
3199	Cotton n.e.s.	2,220.75	2,671.47	2,670.99	2,448.42	2,680.63	120.30	33.00	39.89
44003	Jute cuttings	803.19	950.46	750.23	–	1,353.75	118.34	0.75	0.89
4005	Mesta	942.97	1,176.84	1,176.84	–	–	124.80	0.39	0.49
4099	Jute n.e.s.	1,279.37	1,444.95	1,398.78	1,662.82	1,453.27	112.94	64.94	73.69
Section 2								99.53	115.30
1901	Leather, sheepskin	575.29	495.51	495.51	–	–	86.13	1.79	2.66
1903	Leather, goatskin	435.07	183.92	183.92	–	–	42.27	1.27	0.93
1912	Leather, chrome	151.66	196.74	194.62	–	698.90	129.72	1.10	2.46
1999	Leather n.e.s.	190.27	219.19	219.19	–	–	115.20	1.03	2.05
1301	Cotton yarn, un-bleached 1-20	1.62	1.63	–	–	1.63	100.62	4.76	8.26
1302	Cotton yarn, un-bleached 21-34	1.74	1.51	1.97	–	1.49	86.78	1.35	2.02
1399	Cotton yarn, un bleached n.e.s.	1.92	1.49	1.88	–	1.48	77.60	8.57	11.47
1402	Cotton yarn, bleached 21-34	1.52	1.45	–	–	1.45	95.39	4.76	7.83
1499	Cotton yarn and twist n.e.s.	1.71	3.23	2.58	–	3.24	188.89	10.28	33.50
3402	Jute hessian cloth	0.57	1.42	0.60	–	1.45	249.12	4.98	21.40
6101	Jute gunny bags	1,189.30	1,098.03	1,098.03	–	–	92.33	18.08	28.80
Section 6								57.97	121.38
1799	Medical instruments	2.52	9.02	2.31	–	21.64	357.94	43.21	320.95
4411	Footballs, complete n.e.s.	41.64	82.00	82.00	–	–	196.93	0.24	0.98
4418	Tennis rackets	28.70	59.20	59.20	–	–	206.27	3.82	16.35
4499	Sports goods, n.e.s.	25.61	27.22	27.22	–	–	106.29	0.92	2.03
Section 8								48.19	340.31

TABLE II-22

Unit Prices of Pakistan's Exports to the EBC's and the World, 1965/66

(Rs per unit)

Code (1)		World (3)	EBC's (4)	East Europe (5)	U.S.S.R. (6)	China (7)	EBC price as % of World $(8) = \frac{(4)}{(3)} \times 100$	% Weight in EBC Section Total (9)	Adjusted EBC Price as % of World: By Intra-section Weight (10)
042201	Rice, not in husk, fine	1,002.04	982.42	1,109.65	962.59	—	98.04	99.95	98.04
Section 0								99.95	98.04
262101	Raw wool, greasy	2.54	2.92	—	2.92	—	114.96	3.86	4.56
263199	Raw cotton, n. e. s.	2,375.83	2,658.63	2,590.00	2,436.78	2,700.22	111.90	33.53	38.55
264003	Jute cuttings	710.08	672.51	684.20	776.42	665.24	94.71	1.76	1.71
264004	Jute waste	801.32	889.24	894.34	—	754.00	110.97	0.02	0.02
264005	Mesta	968.52	1,015.17	1,005.13	1,472.31	1,317.00	104.82	0.95	1.02
264006	Mesta cuttings	713.34	695.92	691.63	—	1,121.00	97.56	0.03	0.03
264009	Jute n.e.s.	1,173.53	902.57	1,298.78	324.92	1,200.09	76.91	57.19	45.19
Section 2								97.34	91.08
611901	Leather, sheepskin	511.68	331.43	331.43	—	—	64.77	0.54	0.35
611903	Leather, goatskin	561.65	643.03	620.84	736.39	—	114.49	1.47	1.71
611912	Leather, chrome	286.80	320.15	320.15	—	—	111.63	0.24	0.27
611999	Leather n.e.s.	276.48	157.83	156.01	—	599.00	57.09	0.11	0.06

Code	Item							
652202	Sheets, bed, mill-made	5.12	10.00	—	10.00	—	195.31	0.0001	0.0002
652224	Prints	0.81	0.88	0.86	0.88	—	108.64	6.59	7.26
652299	Cotton cloth, unbleached n. e. s.	0.84	0.84	0.66	0.97	0.61	100.00	6.25	6.34
653402	Jute hessian cloth	0.89	0.68	0.44	—	0.69	76.40	7.18	5.56
653499	Fabrics of jute	1.17	0.65	—	—	0.65	55.56	1.23	0.69
656101	Gunny bags jute	1,599.25	1,539.40	1,457.92	1,664.02	1,702.59	96.26	50.83	49.61
Section 6								98.63	97.61
851001	Leather boots & shoes	0.92	4.17	—	4.17	—	453.26	1.45	10.13
851003	Leather slippers	4.18	4.43	10.55	2.47	—	105.98	13.63	22.27
851005	Footwear n. e. s.	1.80	3.44	3.44	—	—	191.11	1.96	5.78
861201	Goggles & sunglasses	4.31	4.31	7.51	3.68	—	100.00	36.17	55.77
861204	Spectacles n.e.s.	1.88	1.00	1.00	—	—	53.19	0.05	0.04
861799	Medical instruments n.e.s.	2.37	3.03	3.00	3.00	3.04	127.85	2.21	4.36
894403	Badminton rackets n.e.s.	13.92	51.53	51.53	—	—	370.19	6.24	35.62
894417	Tennis balls	42.32	78.25	78.25	—	—	184.90	0.02	0.06
894418	Tennis rackets	30.43	33.56	33.56	—	—	110.29	1.55	2.64
894499	Sports goods n. e. s.	24.88	62.90	62.90	—	—	252.81	1.57	6.12
Section 8								64.85	142.79

TABLE II-23

Unit Prices of Pakistan's Exports to the EBC's and the World, 1966/67

(Rs per unit)

Code (1)	Commodity (2)	World (3)	EBC's (4)	East Europe (5)	U.S.S.R. (6)	China (7)	EBC price as % of World (8) = $\frac{(4)}{(3)}$ x 100	% Weight as in EBC Section Total (9)	Adjusted EBC Price as % of World by Intra-section Weight (10)
042201	Rice, not in the husk, fine	987.08	968.62	964.01	968.84	—	98.13	98.47	98.13
Section 0								98.47	98.13
263101	Cotton, American s-g	2,425.15	2,345.33	2,135.40	2,428.28	2,442.27	96.71	16.85	46.51
263103	Cotton, Desi s-g	1,863.85	2,052.33	2,308.77	—	2,043.67	110.11	6.45	20.27
263109	Cotton, raw n.e.s.	2,112.43	2,375.51	2,345.90	—	2,398.57	112.45	11.74	37.68
Section 2								35.04	104.46
611902	Leather, lambskin	518.53	336.91	336.91	—	—	64.97	1.76	2.19
611911	Leather, goatskin	646.43	680.17	706.98	618.15	960.00	105.22	4.78	9.61
611952	Leather, crome	375.05	508.21	432.58	754.17	—	135.50	1.66	4.30
611959	Leather n.e.s.	378.17	184.00	—	—	184.00	48.66	0.003	0.003
651301	Cotton yarn, unbleached 1-20	1.41	1.56	1.56	—	—	110.64	1.04	2.20
651302	Cotton yarn, unbleached 21-34	1.89	1.62	1.63	—	1.26	85.71	2.54	4.16
651311	Cotton thread, unbleached	1.73	1.15	1.15	—	—	66.47	0.10	0.13
651402	Cotton yarn, bleached 21-34	1.53	1.61	1.62	—	—	105.23	4.63	9.31
651426	Cotton thread for sewing	2.39	2.12	2.12	—	—	88.70	0.33	0.56
651499	Cotton twist & yarn n.e.s.	1.68	1.57	1.59	—	1.49	3.45	1.82	3.25
652122	Cotton sheeting, unbleached	0.68	0.72	0.72	—	—	105.88	0.57	1.15

652244	Cotton drills and jeans	0.92	0.94	0.94	—	—	102.17	0.04	0.08
652246	Cotton poplin	0.97	0.98	0.98	0.98	—	101.03	0.81	1.56
652247	Cotton print	0.91	0.88	0.93	0.87	—	96.70	9.08	16.78
652248	Cotton sheeting, bleached	0.77	1.01	1.01	—	—	131.17	0.13	0.33
652259	Cotton cloth, bleached n.e.s.	0.90	0.83	0.75	1.53	—	92.22	13.62	24.00
656101	Jute gunny bags	1,559.25	1,644.87	2,466.22	—	1,622.43	105.49	7.66	15.44
Section 6								52.33	99.11
841103	Shirts & bush shirts	9.48	16.03	—	16.03	—	169.09	7.55	13.58
841109	Outergarments for men	38.15	12.04	—	12.04	—	31.56	1.25	0.42
841251	Clothing accessories	7.48	12.49	—	12.49	—	166.98	2.48	4.40
841441	Knitted fabrics	8.45	11.70	—	11.70	—	138.46	4.84	7.13
851001	Leather boots & shoes	9.55	16.83	16.81	16.84	7.18	176.23	53.58	100.43
851002	Leather sandals	5.33	14.80	—	14.80	—	277.52	1.60	1.60
851003	Leather slippers	4.69	16.92	—	16.92	—	360.77	0.68	2.61
851009	Leather footwear n.e.s.	5.39	18.86	—	18.86	—	349.91	2.86	10.64
861211	Frames for spectacles	5.42	5.82	9.72	5.39	—	107.38	5.96	6.81
861709	Medical instruments	2.82	4.25	3.00	3.00	4.41	150.71	6.97	11.71
894435	Footballs, complete	76.06	132.26	132.26	—	—	173.89	2.12	3.92
894447	Tennis rackets	29.80	43.07	43.07	—	—	144.53	2.97	4.57
894452	Volley balls, complete	79.85	75.95	75.95	—	—	95.12	1.16	1.17
Section 8								94.02	168.99

TABLE II-24

Unit Prices of Pakistan's Exports to the EBC's and the World, 1967/68

(Rs per unit)

Code (1)	Commodity (2)	World (3)	EBC's (4)	East Europe (5)	U.S.S.R. (6)	China (7)	EBC Price as % of World (8) $=\frac{(4)}{(3)} \times 100$	% Weight in EBC Section Total (9)	Adjusted EBC Price as % of World: by Intra-section Weight (10)
042201	Rice, not in the husk, fine	1,254.91	1,173.02	—	1,173.02	—	93.47	98.53	93.47
Section 0							93.47	98.53	93.47
263101	Cotton, American R.G.	1,925.54	2,778.10	2,924.27	2,437.26	2,719.37	144.28	28.38	41.25
263103	Cotton, Desi R.G.	2,120.69	2,328.30	2,438.91	—	2,466.55	109.79	8.57	9.48
263109	Cotton, raw n.e.s.	2,041.21	2,009.54	1,625.06	—	2,171.10	98.45	1.39	1.38
264001	Jute n.e.s.	1,145.04	1,380.74	1,359.39	1,513.00	1,376.13	120.58	60.24	73.17
264011	Jute cuttings	439.86	654.35	654.35	—	—	148.76	0.66	0.99
264021	Jute waste	754.49	1,044.15	1,044.15	—	—	138.39	0.03	0.04
Section 2								99.27	126.31
611409	Leather, tanned n.e.s.	410.88	529.90	602.50	495.06	—	128.97	1.13	1.83
611902	Leather, sheepskin	238.31	325.17	325.17	—	—	136.45	1.52	2.61
611911	Leather, goatskin	529.72	574.77	654.79	474.18	—	108.50	6.86	9.37
611952	Leather, crome	302.15	546.66	345.88	593.77	—	180.92	0.67	1.53
611959	Leather n.e.s.	213.57	549.51	414.50	549.93	—	257.30	1.04	3.37
651301	Cotton yarn, unbleached 1-20	1.29	1.58	1.60	—	1.22	122.48	0.85	1.31
651302	Cotton yarn, unbleached 21-34	1.54	1.83	1.89	—	1.43	118.83	0.41	0.61
651305	Cotton yarn unbleached (double) 1-20	1.37	1.54	1.54	—	—	112.41	0.89	1.26
651306	Cotton yarn unbleached (double) 21-34	1.64	2.79	—	2.79	—	170.12	0.07	0.15
651309	Cotton yarn, unbleached n.e.s.	1.73	2.35	2.35	—	—	135.84	0.38	0.65
651401	Cotton yarn, bleached 1-20	1.30	1.56	1.52	2.65	—	120.00	4.91	7.42

Code	Item								
651402	Cotton yarn, bleached 21-34	1.49	2.01	2.01	2.01	—	134.90	1.15	1.95
651403	Cotton yarn, bleached 35-47	2.02	2.40	2.18	2.79	—	118.81	0.22	0.33
651404	Cotton yarn, bleached 48+	1.72	1.72	1.73	1.71	—	100.00	0.53	0.67
651406	Cotton yarn, bleached double 21-34	1.82	2.38	2.09	2.64	—	130.77	2.87	4.72
651426	Cotton thread, sewing	2.51	3.56	3.57	2.57	—	141.83	2.36	4.21
651499	Cotton twist & yarn n.e.s.	1.61	2.16	1.77	2.55	—	134.16	2.59	4.37
652122	Cotton sheeting, unbleached	0.63	0.70	0.70	—	—	111.11	11.55	16.15
652129	Cotton cloth, unbleached n.e.s.	0.69	0.72	0.72	—	—	104.35	10.76	14.13
652244	Cotton drills and jeans	0.94	1.19	1.19	—	—	126.60	0.01	0.02
652247	Cotton print	0.90	1.03	0.89	1.03	—	114.44	11.58	16.68
652248	Cotton sheeting, bleached	0.68	0.89	0.89	—	—	130.88	0.12	0.20
652259	Cotton cloth, bleached n.e.s.	0.72	0.81	0.79	0.88	—	112.50	15.22	21.55
653402	Jute hessian cloth	1,487.21	1,819.15	1,819.15	—	—	122.32	0.73	1.12
656901	Curtains	61.86	200.00	200.00	—	—	323.31	0.0003	0.001
656908	Towels	17.10	27.58	27.89	27.53	—	161.29	1.04	2.11
Section 6								79.46	118.32
841102	Pants	28.83	26.94	—	26.94	—	93.44	0.77	0.75
841431	Undergarments	10.45	14.22	—	14.22	—	136.08	1.51	2.14
841441	Knitted fabrics	13.38	22.76	—	22.76	—	170.10	5.66	10.02
851001	Leather boots & shoes	13.12	16.57	16.28	16.68	—	126.30	74.90	98.45
851003	Leather slippers	5.18	20.00	20.00	—	—	386.10	0.29	1.17
861211	Frames for spectacles	6.26	6.30	8.31	3.36	—	100.64	9.66	10.12
861709	Medical instruments	2.88	3.86	4.33	3.00	—	134.03	1.53	2.13
894435	Footballs, complete	77.38	130.37	130.37	—	—	168.48	2.43	4.26
894441	Hockey sticks	51.07	67.83	67.83	—	—	132.82	0.01	0.01
894447	Tennis rackets	28.53	64.90	64.90	—	—	227.48	0.10	0.24
Section 8								96.09	128.54

TABLE II-25

Unit Prices of Pakistan's Exports to the EBC's and the World, 1968/69

(Rs per unit)

Code (1)	Commodity (2)	World (3)	EBC's (4)	East Europe (5)	U.S.S.R. (6)	China (7)	EBC Price as % of World (8)=(4)/(3) x 100	% Weight in EBC Section Total (9)	Adjusted EBC Price as % of World: by Intrasection Weight (10)
032015	Shrimps, canned	154.16	61.39	61.39	–	–	39.82	1.05	0.42
042201	Rice, not in the husk, fine	1,266.23	1,109.24	1,210.90	1,068.94	–	87.60	97.40	86.67
Section 0								98.45	87.09
111002	Icewater & snow	1.23	1.44	–	1.44	–	117.07	29.01	117.07
Section 1								29.01	117.07
262201	Raw wool, scoured	1.63	1.97	1.29	2.37	–	120.86	2.78	6.23
263101	Cotton, American R. G.	2,430.75	2,527.75	2,474.44	2,541.47	2,613.68	103.99	26.85	51.77
263102	Cotton, American S. G.	2,557.11	2,580.35	2,687.48	2,590.66	2,450.49	100.91	17.89	33.47
263103	Cotton, Desi R. G.	2,447.94	2,705.61	2,416.67	–	2,736.00	110.53	5.15	10.55
264001	Jute n. e. s.	1,419.09	1,478.18	1,475.08	1,704.96	1,362.76	104.16	0.43	0.83
264011	Jute cutting	545.78	735.60	735.60	–	–	134.78	0.82	2.05
26402	Jute waste	673.38	428.60	428.60	–	–	63.65	0.01	0.01
Section 2								53.93	104.91
611401	Leather, cow hides	269.83	694.19	1,104.42	674.65	–	257.27	0.49	1.28
611409	Leather, tanned	426.48	499.37	483.21	576.85	–	117.09	2.23	2.66
611902	Leather, sheepskin	592.46	448.42	448.42	–	–	75.69	1.54	1.19
611911	Leather, goatskin	601.06	713.29	743.23	641.19	–	118.67	8.23	9.95
611952	Leather, crome	311.75	403.28	403.28	–	–	129.36	0.02	0.03
611959	Leather, n.e.s.	567.88	823.56	823.56	–	–	145.02	0.02	0.03
651301	Cotton yarn, unbleached 1-20	1.29	1.48	1.48	–	1.22	114.73	0.81	0.95

651302	Cotton yarn, unbleached 21-34	1.51	1.52	1.56	—	1.51	100.66	3.75	3.85
651303	Cotton yarn, unbleached 35-47	2.21	2.42	2.35	—	2.78	109.50	0.50	0.56
651305	Cotton yarn, unbleached (double) 1-20	1.42	1.52	1.52	—	—	107.04	0.13	0.14
651306	Cotton yarn, unbleached (double) 21-34	1.67	1.56	1.56	—	1.57	93.41	1.26	1.20
651307	Cotton yarn, unbleached (double) 35-47	2.17	1.24	1.24	—	—	57.14	0.10	0.06
651309	Cotton yarn, unbleached n. e. s.	1.67	2.35	1.82	—	2.40	140.72	0.41	0.59
651401	Cotton yarn, bleached 1-20	1.36	1.48	1.48	—	—	108.82	2.82	3.13
651402	Cotton yarn, bleached 21-34	1.55	1.64	1.61	—	—	105.81	4.18	4.51
651403	Cotton yarn, bleached 35-47	2.25	2.35	2.35	—	—	104.44	0.26	0.28
651405	Cotton yarn, bleached (double) 1-20	1.22	1.08	1.08	—	—	88.52	0.26	0.23
651406	Cotton yarn, bleached (double) 21-34	1.77	1.89	1.83	2.42	2.18	106.78	4.35	4.73
651426	Cotton thread for sewing	2.44	2.95	2.95	—	—	120.90	0.13	0.16
651499	Cotton yarn and twist n. e. s.	1.72	1.54	1.54	—	—	89.53	0.12	0.11
652122	Cotton sheeting, unbleached	0.64	0.70	0.70	—	—	109.38	8.35	9.31
652129	Cotton cloth, unbleached n. e. s.	0.70	1.11	1.11	—	—	158.57	15.22	24.59
652246	Cotton poplin	0.94	0.97	0.97	—	—	103.19	0.04	0.04
652247	Cotton prints	0.91	1.14	1.14	1.15	—	125.27	7.48	9.55
652248	Cotton sheeting, bleached	0.67	0.72	0.65	0.96	—	107.46	2.78	3.04
652258	Cotton cloth, bleached n. e. s.	0.68	0.62	0.62	—	—	91.18	0.20	0.19
652259	Cotton cloth, bleached n. e. s.	0.77	0.79	0.77	0.92	—	102.60	17.72	18.52
653402	Jute hessian cloth	1,915.26	1,837.10	1,837.92	—	1,608.44	95.92	3.66	3.58
653403	Jute sacking cloth	1,224.62	1,130.80	1,130.80	—	—	92.34	0.07	0.07
653409	Fabrics of jute	2,359.71	1,674.47	2,040.96	1,027.00	—	70.96	0.11	0.08

(Continued)

TABLE II-25 (Continued)

Code (1)	Commodity (2)	World (3)	EBC's (4)	East Europe (5)	U.S.S.R. (6)	China (7)	EBC Price as % of World (8)=(4)/(3) x 100	% Weight in EBC Section Total (9)	Adjusted EBC Price as % of World: by Intrasection Weight (10)
656111	Jute bags	1,051.66	992.10	977.60	1,027.86	—	94.34	0.72	0.69
656112	Jute gunny bags	1,099.82	1,129.99	1,173.38	1,026.58	1,261.27	102.74	1.82	1.91
656113	Jute bags	1,420.57	1,806.86	1,806.86	—	—	127.19	0.29	0.38
656119	Sacks of jute	1,122.39	1,222.14	1,222.28	—	1,037.33	108.89	3.72	4.13
656129	Bags of textile materials	1,148.16	1,356.74	1,356.74	—	—	118.17	0.52	0.63
656908	Towels	14.52	26.56	25.61	26.57	—	182.92	2.72	5.07
657501	Carpets, wool	11.38	8.29	8.29	—	—	72.85	0.67	0.50
657509	Carpets, knotted	10.63	11.15	11.15	—	—	104.89	0.42	0.45
Section 6								98.15	118.37
841441	Knitted fabrics	16.22	20.01	—	20.01	—	123.37	0.57	0.86
851001	Leather boots & shoes	13.86	18.54	19.01	18.07	—	133.77	72.10	117.62
851002	Leather sandals	4.70	18.86	—	18.86	—	401.28	0.04	0.20
851009	Leather footwear n.e.s.	9.45	18.54	17.96	19.03	—	196.19	2.45	5.86
851013	Footwear, other soles	2.00	20.53	20.60	18.86	—	1026.50	1.74	21.78
861211	Frames for spectacles	4.66	4.65	12.53	4.27	—	99.79	3.23	3.93
861709	Medical instruments	2.76	2.19	4.93	0.91	0.89	79.35	1.87	1.81
Section 8								82.00	152.06

TABLE II-26

Unit Prices of Pakistan's Exports to the EBC's and the World, 1969/70

(Rs per unit)

Code (1)	Commodity (2)	World	EBC's	East Europe	U.S.S.R.	China	EBC Price as % of World (8)=$\frac{(4)}{(3)}$ x 100	% Weight in EBC Section Total (9)	Adjusted EBC Price as % of World: by Intrasection Weight (10)
032014	Prawns, canned	296.12	254.41	254.41	—	—	85.91	0.04	0.42
032015	Shrimps, canned	302.00	313.96	313.96	—	—	103.96	7.37	92.53
081305	Oilcake, linseed	17.85	17.85	17.89	—	—	100.22	0.87	10.53
Section 0								8.28	103.48
121004	Tobacco leaf, Virginia	3.71	3.91	3.91	—	—	105.39	63.90	67.36
121009	Tobacco, unmanufactured	2.39	1.60	1.60	—	—	66.95	36.07	24.16
Section 1								99.97	91.52
262201	Wool, raw scoured	1.80	2.21	1.58	2.30	—	122.78	2.13	3.34
263101	Cotton, American R.G.	2,412.21	2,572.85	2,568.98	3,889.51	2,485.01	106.66	4.66	6.34
263102	Cotton, American S.G.	2,629.98	2,691.05	2,671.79	3,719.17	2,719.17	102.32	16.55	21.61
263103	Cotton, Desi R.G.	2,601.94	2,534.57	2,504.33	—	2,539.46	97.41	2.10	2.61
263104	Cotton, Desi S.G.	2,527.30	2,485.56	—	—	2,485.56	98.35	0.94	1.18
263109	Cotton raw n.e.s.	2,626.68	2,669.77	2,664.19	—	2,602.98	101.64	3.44	4.46
264001	Jute n.e.s.	1,381.28	1,399.35	1,377.33	1,497.06	1,369.92	101.31	46.48	60.10
264011	Jute cuttings	513.32	554.35	555.82	—	447.33	107.99	0.78	1.08
264021	Jute waste	486.93	539.76	539.76	—	—	110.85	0.05	0.07
283905	Chromium	133.24	131.53	130.63	—	137.55	98.72	1.22	1.54
Section 2								78.35	102.33

(Continued)

111

TABLE II-26 (Continued)

Code (1)	Commodity (2)	World	EBC's	Europe	U.S.S.R.	China	EBC Price as % of World (8)=(4)÷(3) x 100	% Weight in EBC Section Total (9)	Adjusted EBC Price as % of World: by Intrasection Weight (10)
611401	Leather of cow hide	235.77	210.85	210.85	—	—	83.09	3.99	3.67
611402	Leather of buffalo hide	269.58	262.67	262.67	—	—	97.44	0.15	0.16
611409	Leather, tanned n. e. s.	302.14	775.00	775.00	—	—	256.50	0.01	0.03
611902	Leather, sheepskin	637.92	663.78	662.69	682.14	—	104.05	2.95	3.40
611911	Leather, goatskin	563.64	770.13	781.40	692.60	—	136.64	6.99	10.57
611952	Leather, crome	633.75	284.31	289.78	234.00	—	44.86	0.03	0.01
611959	Leather n. e. s.	376.77	740.71	740.71	—	—	196.59	0.02	0.04
651301	Cotton yarn, unbleached 1-20	1.36	1.58	1.60	—	1.46	116.18	1.84	2.36
651302	Cotton yarn, unbleached 21-34	1.55	1.65	1.63	—	1.67	106.45	5.23	6.16
651303	Cotton yarn, unbleached 35-47	2.07	2.68	—	—	2.68	129.47	0.20	0.29
651305	Cotton yarn, unbleached (double) 1-20	1.52	1.47	1.47	—	—	96.71	0.07	0.07
651306	Cotton yarn, unbleached (double) 21-34	1.72	2.06	1.87	—	2.59	119.77	1.18	1.56
651309	Cotton yarn, unbleached n. e. s.	1.53	1.78	1.75	—	2.77	116.34	0.46	0.59
651401	Cotton yarn, bleached 1-20	1.44	1.59	1.59	—	—	110.42	1.78	2.17
651402	Cotton yarn, bleached 21-34	1.66	1.54	1.54	—	1.39	92.77	6.14	6.30
651403	Cotton yarn, bleached 35-47	2.39	2.39	2.39	—	—	100.00	0.12	0.13
651406	Cotton yarn, bleached (double) 21-34	1.89	1.96	1.96	—	—	103.70	2.12	2.43
651499	Cotton yarn and twist n. e. s.	1.61	1.70	1.72	—	1.55	105.59	1.26	1.47
652122	Cotton sheeting, unbleached	0.71	0.78	0.78	—	—	109.86	7.85	9.54
652129	Cotton cloth, unbleached n. e. s.	0.68	0.72	0.72	1.68	0.54	105.88	16.71	19.57
652137	Cotton shirting, unbleached	0.80	0.65	0.65	—	—	81.25	0.10	0.09
652242	Cotton canvas, bleached	2.37	1.02	—	1.02	—	43.04	0.05	0.02
652244	Cotton drills and jeans	1.03	0.99	0.97	—	2.45	96.12	0.76	0.81

652247	Cotton print	0.93	1.12	—	1.12	2.45	120.43	4.49	5.98
652248	Cotton sheeting, bleached	0.63	0.74	0.70	0.99	—	117.46	1.90	2.47
652251	Cotton suiting	1.69	1.69	—	1.69	—	100.00	0.03	0.03
652254	Cotton shirting, bleached	0.80	0.85	0.85	0.96	—	106.25	1.36	1.60
652255	Cotton shirting, bleached, handloom	0.92	1.00	1.00	—	—	108.70	0.09	0.11
652259	Cotton cloth, bleached n.e.s.	0.78	0.75	0.75	—	1.01	96.15	8.93	9.50
652262	Cotton sarees, bleached	0.95	0.94	—	0.94	—	98.95	0.01	0.01
653402	Jute hessian cloth	1,904.51	1,793.87	1,792.30	—	1,873.38	94.19	2.49	2.59
653403	Jute sacking cloth	1,341.74	1,205.02	1,160.93	—	1,982.54	89.81	0.11	0.11
653409	Jute fabrics	2,066.74	1,855.15	1,855.15	—	—	89.77	0.29	0.29
656111	Jute bags	1,149.70	1,041.83	—	—	1,041.83	90.62	0.35	0.35
656112	Jute gunny bags	1,128.54	1,234.47	1,263.65	—	1,086.09	109.39	1.52	1.84
656113	Jute hessian bags	1,674.04	1,669.53	1,673.04	—	1,015.89	99.73	0.52	0.57
656119	Sacks of jute	1,099.23	1,245.79	1,277.49	—	1,020.49	113.33	1.17	1.47
656901	Curtains	91.47	100.04	—	100.04	—	109.47	0.07	0.08
656908	Towels	12.75	21.07	—	21.07	—	165.25	5.23	9.56
656911	Linens n.e.s	59.62	60.01	—	60.01	—	100.65	0.14	0.16
657501	Carpets, wool	10.73	6.82	6.76	20.00	19.88	63.56	1.84	1.29

(Continued)

113

TABLE II-26 (Continued)

Code (1)	Commodity (2)	World	EBC's	Europe	U.S.S.R.	China	EBC Price as % of World (8)=(4)/(3) x 100	% Weight in EBC Section Total (9)	Adjusted EBC Price as % of World: by Intrasection Weight (10)
657503	Rugs, wool	12.71	10.00	—	—	10.00	78.68	0.001	0.0001
657509	Carpets, knotted	10.19	9.81	9.81	—	—	96.27	0.14	0.15
Section 6								90.39	109.60
841102	Pants	96.70	99.09	—	99.09	—	102.47	3.09	3.24
841103	Shirts & bush shirts	17.39	39.37	59.84	37.68	—	226.39	6.39	14.78
841109	Outergarments for men	42.90	126.09	157.71	125.60	—	293.92	4.78	14.36
841119	Outergarments for women	97.94	115.59	311.67	99.12	—	118.02	0.44	0.53
841411	Sacks	74.42	74.42	—	—	74.42	100.00	0.03	0.03
841421	Outergarments, knitted	7.71	6.49	—	6.49	—	84.18	3.45	2.97
841441	Knitted fabrics	18.93	140.95	—	140.69	448.11	744.59	10.93	83.17
851001	Leather boots & shoes	12.13	18.11	13.75	18.60	—	149.30	44.44	67.81
851002	Leather sandals	5.17	20.00	—	—	20.00	386.85	0.0001	0.0004
851003	Leather slippers	5.04	14.85	—	14.85	—	294.64	0.42	1.26
851009	Leather footwear n. e. s.	8.41	22.27	—	22.27	—	264.80	0.84	2.27
851013	Footwear, other soles	2.19	8.23	16.02	7.91	—	375.80	10.66	40.94
861211	Frames for spectacles	8.06	8.12	10.69	7.91	—	100.74	10.00	10.22
861212	Parts of spectacle frames	18.19	10.00	10.00	—	—	54.98	0.04	0.02
861709	Medical instruments	3.19	4.59	4.59	—	—	143.89	0.47	0.69
861713	Surgical instruments n.e.s.	2.65	1.73	11.17	1.00	5.04	65.28	0.61	0.41
894412	Badminton rackets	14.81	42.66	42.66	—	—	288.05	0.53	1.56
894441	Hockey balls	40.01	59.52	59.52	—	—	148.76	0.02	0.03
894435	Footballs, complete	62.59	151.60	151.60	—	—	242.21	0.05	0.12
894441	Hockey sticks	57.01	75.55	75.55	—	—	132.52	0.01	0.01
894447	Tennis rackets	35.58	108.62	108.62	—	—	305.28	0.20	0.62
894499	Sports goods, n. e. s.	37.15	56.20	59.45	45.78	55.99	151.28	0.55	0.85
Section 8								97.85	245.89

114

TABLE II-27

Jute Trading Corporation Sales of PTC (Pakistan
Tossa, Grade C) and PWC (Pakistan, White,
Grade C) to Selected West and East
European Countries, 1969/70
(£s per bale)

Country	No. of Bales	Average PTC	Price PWC
West Europe			
Britain	36,635	125	123
Belgium	20,979	123	122
Germany	16,721	126	—
France	3,196	—	120
East Europe			
Poland	29,798	131	132
Czechoslovakia	13,583	131	129

Source: Jute Trading Corporation.

TABLE II-28

F.O.B. Prices of Substations for the Water and Power Development Agency's (WAPDA's) 132/11 KV 22-Grid Station Project
(thousand rupees)

Country	Grid Station with 10 MVA Transformer	In-Out Station with 10 MVA Transformer
Bulgaria	—	597.3
Poland	564.2	786.2
Yugoslavia	485.1	694.9
Average East Europe	524.7	692.8
Britain (Reyrolle)	754.7	986.5
Germany (BBC)	576.9	906.5
France (Cogelex)	567.2	770.3
Denmark (Elagwa)	594.1	730.7
Average Western Europe	623.2	848.5

Source: WAPDA, Lahore.

116

TABLE II-29

F.O.B. Prices of Power Transformers for
WAPDA's 22-Grid Station Project
(thousand rupees)

Country	10 MVA 132/11 KV	20 MVA 132/11 KV	30 MVA 132/66 KV
Bulgaria	201.5	—	—
Poland	226.5	300.0	321.5
Yugoslavia (Energoinvest)	241.4	315.4	415.8
Average East Europe	223.0	305.1	368.7
Britain (Reyrolle)	331.3	463.6	561.5
Germany (BBC)	281.3	353.4	521.4
France (Cogelex)	297.0	368.0	439.0
Italy (Savigliano)	285.0	353.0	548.0
Average Western Europe	298.7	384.5	517.9

Source: WAPDA, Lahore.

TABLE II-30

C.I.F. Price of Cotton Textile Spinning Machinery for Basic 12,500-Spindle Unit with Necessary Back Processing Machinery
(thousand $)

Britain	919.4
Germany	1,071.7
Italy	933.6
Switzerland	1,139.3
Japan	720.9
Average West	957.0
U.S.S.R	654.6

Note: Backing processing machinery includes blow room machinery; carding engines; drawing, roving, and spinning frames selected to make a balanced unit.

Source: Industrial Development Bank of Pakistan.

TABLE II.31

Zinc Imports Through the Trading Corporation of Pakistan, 1967/68-1969/70
(£'s per ton)

Date	Source	Name of allocation	Price Paid	LME Cash Price[a]	Tied Source Premium (%)
(1)	(2)	(3)	(4)	(5)	(6)
Nov. 16, 1967	North Korea	Barter	105.0	99.125-99.25	105.9
Dec. 12, 1968	Australia	Cash-cum-bonus	115.0	114.25-114.75	100.6
Jan. 9, 1969	U.S.S.R.	Barter	127.3[b]	115.50-115.75	110.1
Feb. 17, 1969	North Korea	Barter	124.6[b]	112.25-112.375	110.9
May 10, 1969	U.S.S.R.	Barter	134.2[b]	118.25-118.50	113.4
July 23, 1969	North Korea	Barter	129.3[b]	119.375-119.50	108.3
Jan. 17, 1970	Canada	Credit	134.7[c] CTG 132.8[c] KHI	124-124.50	108.4 106.9
Mar. 26, 1970	Canada	Credit	137.0[c] CTG 135.2[c] KHI	123-123.25	111.3 109.8
June 15, 1970	Canada	Credit	126.6[c]	121.25-121.50	104.3
June 1, 1970	U.S.S.R.	Barter	141.9[b]	121.50-121.75	116.6

Notes: [a] Pounds per long ton 1967-69; pounds per metric ton 1970.
[b] Rupees converted at Rs 11.4=£1
[c] Canadian dollars converted at C$2.59=£1

Source: TCP, Metal Bulletin, Delivery at Chittagong, East Pakistan and Karachi, West Pakistan.

TABLE II-32

Estimated Future Debt Service Payments to EBC's on External Public Debt Outstanding on June 30, 1969

(thousand $)

	1969/70	1970/71	1971/72	1972/73	1973/74	1974/75	1975/76	1976/77	1977/78	1978/79	1979/80
China	—	—	—	—	686	686	6,141	6,141	6,141	6,141	10,417
Czechoslovakia	4,949	5,264	5,268	5,173	5,078	4,983	3,899	2,780	2,736	2,324	2,200
Poland	1,340	1,394	1,364	1,334	1,305	1,275	1,162	904	735	165	—
Russia	10,141	16,364	21,400	15,639	8,874	8,194	7,694	6,945	6,196	4,100	1,324
Yugoslavia	9,806	10,314	11,960	11,376	10,612	8,532	6,413	5,706	4,860	3,319	1,383
Total	26,236	33,336	39,992	33,522	26,555	23,670	25,309	22,476	20,668	16,049	15,324

Source: International Bank for Reconstruction and Development, Current Economic Position and Prospects of Pakistan, Vol. II: Statistical Appendix, (Report No. SA - 15a) (Washington: IBRD, July 17, 1970), Table 4. 2.

APPENDIXES

A

The economic development of backward countries became a problem in Western analysis only after World War II, some time after it had emerged as a problem in practice. Until then the future seemed well taken care of: Capitalism would reach into the outermost bounds of the earth in search of raw materials and trade outlets. It would sap the self-sufficiency of the local economies wherever it went, and would draw them into systematic contact with the world market.

On occassion, it would be bloody, and civilized men guarding the uncertain marches between purposive violence and brutality might be shamed. But they would not denounce the system for that alone, for the mission it was pursuing with its boots was a civilizing one, absolutely in the canon of the classical political economists, relatively in Marx. It was bringing to the entire world the benign influence of capitalism's superior productivity and leading mankind to a common heritage.

These civilized men were wrong, and by the mid- to late 1940's they were said to be wrong, not only by the Marxist and other subcultures of political criticism, but by the main body of academic economists concerned with development.

The capitalist system certainly grew, but not always—not, for instance, during the two world wars and the intervening depression.

This Appendix, which first appeared in New Society, March 4, 1971, develops some of the political arguments touched on in the introduction.

123

It did wrench the backward countries into alignment with the world market, but it also stopped them from fully entering it.

The cheap materials that poured out of the modern mining and plantation enclaves in backward countries did encourage further specialization downstream—in the capitalist heartlands. The demand for equipment, skills, and services for use in these enclaves did the same upstream—again, "at home," not in the host environment. The size of investment, the scale of operation, the experience of social control, all swelled where capitalism was already a going concern.

But everywhere else, indigenous society subsided into increasing agriculturalization and unemployment, a loss of skills and productivity—a spiral of growing backwardness and poverty. Growing futility, too, since the invasion of capitalism had both destroyed the backward countries' social and economic integration, and raised the price of entry into the new system beyond their immediate reach.

So, by the end of the 1940's, the academic mainstream had turned interventionist, almost to a man. Academics prescribed, planned, travelled tirelessly, in the cause of policy. They advised governments to harness to domestic "take-off" the development impulses leaking abroad; they pressed for large initial efforts and therefore for state planning and state enterprise; they masterminded a protracted war on the theory and practice of economic liberalism.

They did not agree on everything. They quarrelled about the extent to which the backward countries could, or should, be protected in the initial stages of their development; the place for foreign capital; the best use of aid; the relative merits of state and private enterprise. More recently a cocky neoliberal minority has struck out alone, impressed by the seemingly irrepressible growth of world trade and the obvious failure of their colleagues.

But, by and large, the postwar orthodoxy has survived. For each country, it goes, there is a pattern of production that would both employ its people, and be reasonably efficient in world terms; governments should create that pattern, alone or with outside help. It is the optimistic, interventionalist orthodoxy, enshrined in McNamara's World Bank, which only last month [February 1971] denied promised funds to Gabon for not having exercised sufficient control over the foreign interests despoiling that country's resources.

There is an Eastern orthodoxy as well. It too has undergone change, although in an opposite direction. As it emerged from the intense Russian debate on industrialization in the mid-1920's, it totally opposed all thought of development through integration with the ruling system of production and trade. On the contrary, if Russia was to avoid military defeat or economic suffocation, or both, at the hands of that system, it would have to withdraw as far as possible from contact with it, exercise the strictest control over what little remained of foreign trade, and pour everything into a huge, broad-based indus- trialization. Implicit in the approach, although not expressed at the time, was the idea that the planned economy would ultimately prove its superiority by winning for Russian industry a place in the world system on Russian terms—that is, as part of an integrated, articulated, and developed national economy.

Long before that stage was reached, however, the early orthodoxy had foundered. The East Europeans rose against its terrible cost in the mid-1950's and won a mite of freedom. A second round is being fought now. Within Russia itself, the threat of economic rundown in impelling the government to open the country more and more to world trade, including trade with the backward countries. And the economists have been forced to rediscover, and commend, the advantages of an international division of labor—the "dynamic comparative advantage" of Western economics.

The new Eastern orthodoxy on development is not like its Western counterpart in all respects. It is more interventionist, more autarkist, more state-capitalist. It deals in longer time spans and larger scale. It is slightly less crippled by academic casuistry, and slightly more by political and social constraints. But it does share the basic assumption of the major Western school—that development is possible in the world we know; that there is something the backward countries themselves can do, with or without outside help, some trick of policy, that can shift the world pattern of production and distribution in their favor, so that they might be absorbed into it as whole societies.

The reality is harsher than that. The minimum cost of entry into the world market is growing every day. The resources from which to fund it in backward countries are not. The relative size of this critical minimum—made up of a minimum development effort (in investment, distribution, education, government, ideology, and so on), and the minimum defense effort on which it is predicated—is the nub of the problem of underdevelopment. Take China, the plain man's best example of a country that can "make it," which has the resources, the discipline, the leadership—everything needed to impose its own amendments on the world—which has already made remarkable material progress since the Communists took over.

China also makes nuclear weapons and the missiles to deliver them. Abhorrent as these are from a socialist or simply humanitarian standpoint, they do make sense in terms of national interest and nationalist ideology as well as in narrow military terms. Technologically, they are obviously an amazing achievement. But from the point of view of economic and social development they are disaster.

The claim has not yet been made that Mao's thoughts are especially effective in smashing atoms, so one can presume that China's scientists, many of whom were trained abroad, use techniques similar to those used in the rest of the world and need resources of a roughly similar order of magnitude. For example, it seems reasonable to suppose that they use as much electricity in the production of fissile material as the Americans used in their first gas diffusion plant at Oak Ridge, Tennessee—some 14.9 billion kilowatt hours a year or 25-50 percent, of total Chinese electricity production in 1964 (depending on whether one accepts Russian or U.S. figures). The Chinese might be using a like proportion of scientists, technicians, and skilled workers; of scarce materials, services, and components. Even if they are not, even if they enjoy all the advantages of latecoming, and do not have to pull skilled workers out of the armed forces, or empty their treasury of silver, or requisition men and machines from other urgent uses, as the Americans did thirty years ago, they must still be diverting a huge proportion of their productive capacity from productive use.

This is not something they can afford to do. The critical minimum development effort is growing as violently as the military one. When Mao took power, a 4- to 5-million ton per year steel plant was exceptional, a 1- to 2-million ton per year plant large. Now the Japanese are setting a floor to viability at 10 to 12 million tons a year. Of course, Chinese steel can be, and is, protected; and so is every single branch of Chinese production.

But the economy as a whole is not, and cannot be. Ultimately, it will have to prove its viability in competition with the rest of the world—economically, if possible, militarily if need be. Or it will collapse.

The scale of the effort needed makes it unlikely that the proof will be forthcoming. Given the alternative, it must be tried. So the Great Leap Forward is followed by the Cultural Revolution, and the Cultural Revolution will no doubt be followed by another gigantic social spasm, and that by another, as the ineluctable necessity to achieve a given initial size pushes the Chinese regime to the limit in gathering and deploying the economic surplus, and to even greater extremes in centralizing the political and social authority to make that possible. All this while propounding devolution and mass involvement.

But there are limits beyond which they dare not step. Once the unity of the country and the continued coherence of the state are called into question, centralization must necessarily stop. And if that happens before it can produce the critical minima, development itself becomes a dream.

China's fate is not an internal Chinese matter. Failure is bound to close the period in which a Russian-type state capitalist development could be thought feasible for backward countries, even if the more orthodox Western variant was not; in which the bloody, treacherous forced march through autarkic industrialization could be thought to constitute progress in some restricted sense; in which the West could find it expedient to temper its savagery here and there, in order to offset the attraction of this "progress."

Above all, failure means the end of a terrible illusion, held as fervently by many seeming revolutionaries as by members of the more orthodox schools: that economic development in backward countries is possible without revolution in the developed; that there is hope of a humane existence for the majority of mankind while the Russo-American system of conflict continues to generate its frightful military and economic pressure waves.

Real optimism hangs on the death of that illusion.

The socialist countries should grant concessions to the developing countries whose advantages are at least equivalent to the effects of preferences that would be granted by the developed countries with market economies.

The socialist countries should:

1. Adopt and implement measures designed to increase the rate of growth of the imports of manufactures and semimanufactures from developing countries, and to diversify such imports in consonance with the latter's trade and development requirements;

2. Undertake to contribute to the maintenance of remunerative and stable prices for the exports of developing countries by the inclusion of suitable provisions in their trade agreements with these countries;

3. In drawing up their national and regional development plans, take due account of the production and export potential in developing countries;

———————————

The Charter of Algiers was adopted in October 1967 at the Ministerial Meeting of the "Group of 77." which formed at the UNCTAD meeting in 1964 (U.N. Conference on Trade and Development, Geneva, March 23-June 16, 1964) in order to present a common Southern Front to the wealthier countries.

4. Abolish customs duties and other trade restrictions on goods imported from and originating in developing countries;

5. Eliminate the margin between the import price and the domestic selling price of the goods imported from developing countries

6. Refrain from re-exporting the goods purchased from developing countries, unless it is with the consent of the developing countrie concerned;

7. Encourage conclusion of industrial branch agreements for the supply of plants and equipment on credit to the developing countries accepting repayment of such credits in particular with the goods manufactured by such plants in the developing countries concerned;

8. Multilateralize, to the extent possible, among the socialist countries of East Europe, payment arrangements with developing countries to facilitate increase of imports from the latter;

9. Grant preferential access conditions for products originating from developing countries; these conditions should include the establishment, in their international purchasing policies, of margins of tolerance in favor of the developing countries with regard to prices and delivery terms;

10. Within the framework of UNCTAD, set up permanent consultative machinery through which socialist countries and developing countries may promote mutual trade and economic cooperation, and solve the problems and obstacles that may arise.

MICHAEL KIDRON, a political economist, is a Senior Research Officer at the Institute of Commonwealth Studies, Oxford University. He has been a Research Adviser to the Pakistan Institute of Development Economics, Karachi; has written on problems of development in South Asia (Foreign Investments in India; Economic Development in South Asia, with E.A.G. Robinson); and travelled widely in the region as well as in East Europe and Russia.

He has taught at the University of Hull, in England, and, as Visiting Professor of Economics, at Bombay University, India, and the University of California (Davis).

Apart from writing on problems of development, he has written Western Capitalism Since the War. He is currently engaged on a study of defense and development in South Asia.